P9-ARY-052

PAYING
FOR YOUR
EDUCATION

OTHER PUBLICATIONS FROM THE COLLEGE BOARD

The College Handbook. Published annually, 1560 pages.

The College Cost Book. Published annually, 192 pages.

Index of Majors. Published annually, 600 pages.

I Can Be Anything: A Career Book for Women. Joyce Slayton Mitchell, 1982, 336 pages.

Choices and Changes: A Career Book for Men. Joyce Slayton Mitchell, 1982, 320 pages.

PAYING FOR YOUR EDUCATION

A Guide for Adult Learners

CARL CAMPBELL BRIGHAM LIBRARY
EDUCATIONAL TESTING SERVICE
PRINCETON, NEW JERSEY 08540

COLLEGE ENTRANCE EXAMINATION BOARD
NEW YORK
1983

The Office of Adult Learning Services (OALS) of the College Board conducts activities to improve adults' access to postsecondary education. The major goals of the office are to provide new programs, training, and publications to support the transition of adults to and from education; help institutions strengthen their capabilities in lifelong education; develop the skills of professionals who serve adults; assemble and disseminate information about adult learning; and advance knowledge in the field of adult learning. To meet these goals, the Office offers advisory services, technical assistance, and training workshops, and produces publications and develops new products.

The College Scholarship Service (CSS) is an activity of the College Board concerned with improving equal educational opportunity. Through the determination of financial need, the CSS helps to distribute financial assistance equitably to students. Its services are offered to students and their parents, to secondary schools, to noncollegiate sponsors of financial aid programs, and to all institutions of postsecondary education.

Operational activities for the College Scholarship Service are performed by Educational Testing Service.

The College Board is a nonprofit membership organization that provides tests and other educational services for students, schools, and colleges. The membership is composed of more than 2,500 colleges, school systems, and education associations. Representatives of the members serve on the Board of Trustees and advisory councils and committees that consider the programs of the College Board and participate in the determination of its policies and activities.

Chapter 3: Adapted, with permission, from *Back to School: The College Guide for Adults*, by William Haponski and Charles E. McCabe. Copyright © 1982, Peterson's Guides, Inc. All rights reserved.

Copyright © 1983 by College Entrance Examination Board. All rights reserved.

Copies of this book may be ordered from: College Board Publications, Box 886, New York, New York 10101. The price is $7.95.

Editorial inquiries concerning this book should be directed to: Editorial Office, The College Board, 888 Seventh Avenue, New York, New York 10106.

Library of Congress Catalog Card Number: 82–73562
Printed in the United States of America

9 8 7 6 5 4 3 2 1

CONTENTS

ACKNOWLEDGMENTS

In this expanded and revised edition, major contributions were made by Kingston Johns, Jr., Ronald Miller, William Haponski, and Charles McCabe, for whose work we are most grateful. We would also like to express our appreciation and thanks for the help and advice received from Ann Diehl, Peter Fishbein, Norman Kurland, Sally Mahon, George Melican, Robert Purga, Michael Scarpelli, Joseph Sciami, Judy Tatum and Jerry Whitlock, all of whom took the time to review the current version in its early stages. The first edition of this guide was developed by Robert Purga, Assistant Director of Adult Learning Services at the New York State Education Department.

Preparation of this guide was a joint undertaking of the Office of Adult Learning Services and the College Scholarship Service. Special credit goes to Pamela Christoffel, Research and Development Associate for the Washington Office of the College Board, who was responsible for the overall coordination of the guide, and to Deborah Kahane, Program Assistant of the Office of Adult Learning Services, who coordinated the preparation of the final draft of the manuscript. Finally, we wish to thank Ronald Miller, who acted as principal reviewer of the final manuscript and also tackled the difficult job of updating and revising the chapter on federal student aid programs.

Carol B. Aslanian
Director
Office of Adult Learning Services

Natala Wickstrom
Vice President
Student Assistance Services

Some of the best things in life are free, but for most kinds of education, you need money. This book will show you how and where to apply for it.

1

How
to
Use
this
Book

The purpose of this book is to help adults find the money to pay for education. Unlike young college students who may be financially dependent on their families, most adults interested in furthering their education are self-supporting, and many of them have dependents of their own. They would like to enroll in degree and nondegree programs, but hold back because they are worried about costs. And rising college costs make it difficult for adult learners to support themselves, their families, and their studies all at the same time. What adult learners often do not know is they *can* qualify for and receive financial aid. Unfortunately, many of them do not know how to go about getting it.

This second edition of *Paying for Your Education* presents new and updated information, including all the current federal grant and loan programs. The United States government is still the largest source of financial aid for students. Despite the recent federal cutbacks in educational grants and loans, some students will continue to receive federal money. If you qualify for any of the federal programs we have listed, be sure to check to see if funding is still available; a number of programs may have been drastically reduced or eliminated. It's important to keep abreast of changes that can affect your getting financial aid. If money *is* available, by all means, apply for it — you have nothing to lose. If you are ineligible for federal funds, we have listed many other sources of financial assistance that may help pay for your education.

If you count yourself among the one out of every five adults in this country involved in continuing education, but are unsure of how to finance it, take advantage of the opportunities outlined in this book. There are many ways to pay for your education. By reading and using the information we have provided, you have already taken the first step in furthering your education.

This book is the most accurate and complete book of its kind. It tells you:

- What financial aid is and who can qualify for it
- How to cut costs in getting a college degree
- What aid is available for part-time study
- How to shop for aid and how to compare financial aid awards
- What steps to take in getting aid and when to take them
- How to keep track of deadlines and critical dates
- Where to find special kinds of aid
- How to apply for admission to college
- Where to get more information and help
- How to understand financial aid language.

There are many types of assistance adults can draw on to help meet the costs of pursuing further education. Consider these examples:

A sales representative for a large industrial firm finances a series of noncredit business courses through his company's fringe benefit plan.

A divorced housewife with two children uses a federal Pell Grant to help her earn a degree in management.

A veteran secures his barber's license while receiving benefits from the GI Bill.

A 68-year-old woman pays no tuition at a state university because her state's legislation exempts students over 65 from tuition payments.

A married engineer uses a loan to complete an advanced degree in engineering. Because he is improving his current job skills, he can claim educational costs as a federal income tax deduction.

These are just a few ways people have used to fit available help to their particular situations. Now, to get the most out of this book, and to help you find the kinds of financial assistance that can work for you, follow these preliminary steps. First, *scan through the book.* See for yourself what it is all about. Get to know where those topics that concern you most are located in the text. Your first task is to become generally familiar with the contents. Next, *spend some time in* Chapter 11, *"Key to Financial Aid Language,"* beginning on page 129. It will help you to better understand this book, the forms and materials you may use later, and some of the administrators with whom you will be communicating. After that, *start at the beginning again.* This time thoroughly read the whole book and complete all of the checklists, guides, and other sections.

If you take these steps and are qualified to enter college, the chances are good that you will be able to pay for your education. *But you must be persistent* in your efforts. Don't think you are too old to be eligible for financial assistance, because you aren't!

One word of caution: the purpose of financial aid is to assist you in achieving your educational goals if you are financially unable to afford the cost of tuition, fees, books, and other expenses related to furthering your education. Do not compromise your educational goals by studying something less desirable or taking courses that are of no interest to you just because you can get financial aid.

Whenever change comes, early or late,
and to whomever it comes, rich or poor,
learning is one way of dealing with it.

2

Life Changes as Reasons for Learning

Almost half of all full-time and part-time college students today are adults. All over the United States and Canada, thousands of self-supporting adults are pursuing postsecondary study, often in new and exciting ways. This adult student body includes working people with little or no college education, career-oriented people who want to acquire special knowledge and skills, college graduates who want to change careers or who want advanced degrees in their fields, women who plan to enter or reenter the work force, retired people who use their leisure time to study, and many others.

Why are so many adults getting a postsecondary education, and why are they returning to formal education at such a rapid rate? The College Board surveyed 2,000 Americans 25 years of age and older to find the answers to those questions and many more. According to the survey, half of *all* American adults studied *something* during the past year! When asked about their reasons for learning, most of the surveyed adults described changes in their lives: career, family, leisure, art, health, religion, and citizenship. Of these adults, 56 percent named career transitions as the reason for deciding to learn, while another 29 percent named transitions in their family and leisure life. Of course, some adults elected to learn for the sake of the learning experience itself. But for most adults, changing circumstances were the chief reasons for learning.

A career change, job promotion, or work relocation frequently requires new skills, which mean more learning. Adults seek to learn what they must in order to succeed in their new situation. For example:

"I worked in a prison as a guard. It was a terrible job and very dangerous. People got killed in the prison and there were riots sometimes. I could not stay in that work. So, I gave it up and enrolled in a nearby college where I'm studying business administration."

"There are good possibilities for advancement in my line of management, but I didn't have a college degree. That could eliminate me from being considered by a lot of companies. Now I am almost through college and have already partici- pated in several corporate recruiting interviews right on campus. Prospects seem good."

"I could move to a better community with good schools for my kids if I could qualify for an open- ing that is coming up in about a year. My wife and I decided it was important to us, so I enrolled in two courses at the community college."

Technological advances in business and industry, the new wave of telecommunications in the work place and professional recertification requirements are among a num- ber of factors that not only mandate but offer opportunities for more education and training. Education can result in more income, better job security, and widened career alternatives.

Family events often trigger the need for learning, as in these cases:

"I got a divorce at about the time my youngest child turned five. I had wanted to go back to school before that, but my husband didn't want me to. He was content that I stay at home. I didn't want to — so that was a bone of contention between us. Then, when I got my divorce, I was able to get away from diapers and dishes. Back to school I went, and with my ambition and some luck, I'll have a paralegal job in six months."

"Another child meant we had to have more income. So, I went job hunting, which showed me that I could not compete effectively with other prospective employees. Now I'm taking a course in construction estimating. And I've found out

*that the supervising engineer plans to bring me
into the main office, give me a promotion, and
raise my salary as soon as I finish the course."*

For millions of adults, education is a good way to re-
solve old problems and to take advantage of new opportunities.

Leisure provides rewarding opportunities for more
learning. For example,

*"I elected to retire early from a supervisory posi-
tion with a major corporation. Now I'm excited
about getting a college degree, something I was
unable to accomplish earlier in life. But I have a
modest income, and I'm not old enough to draw
Social Security benefits yet. A large state university operates a branch in this city. A counselor
there has arranged for credit-by-examination,
told me how to budget most of the costs, and
helped me apply for a loan to cover the immediate
expenses of tuition and fees. If everything happens on schedule, I'll have my degree in about
three years."*

*"When I attended college as a young adult, it
seemed to me that most of the courses were
required. Of course I took them, but few really
interested me. Now that I have retired, the
chance to study what I want feels like a luxury.
Besides, the cost is no greater than what I'd pay
for some recreational activity."*

As Carol Aslanian and Henry Brickell point out in
their book, *Americans in Transition,* more than 80 percent
of adults who learn do so because their lives are changing.
The changes are generally in the areas of career and family.
They think learning is needed to cope with such events as
entering the work force, upgrading skills for promotion,

and dealing with the vacuum created by the death or divorce of a spouse.

Of all those adults who attend an educational institution, the great majority goes to either four-year or two-year colleges. Some enroll at vocational-technical institutes or proprietary schools. We now live in a nation of learners! And you can be one of them.

In 1981–82, nearly $17 billion in financial assistance from federal, state, institutional, and private sources was available to help millions of students meet the costs of post-secondary education or training. It can help you, too. You do not have to be poor to qualify, but you usually have to prove you need money. You'd probably be surprised to learn how many students are eligible for some amount of financial aid, especially at private institutions. In this book, you'll find out about the different types of financial aid, and by following the steps outlined, you can discover whether or not you are eligible for such aid and how to apply for it.

"I want to be ready if life calls on me."

Pearl Bailey, at age 58, on enrolling as a
freshman at Georgetown University to
study for a teaching career.

3

*How
to
Apply
to
College*

Adapted, with permission, from *Back to School: The College Guide for Adults,* by William Haponski
and Charles E. McCabe. Copyright © 1982, Peterson's Guides, Inc. All rights reserved.

Considerations of financial aid are irrelevant, of course, unless you are admitted to a college. But if you are concerned that as an adult you may be at a disadvantage in competing with younger students, be at ease. Large numbers of adults attend college. The National Center for Education Statistics (NCES) reports that, whereas enrollment of traditional students (those under 25) is expected to drop in the 1980s, enrollment of adults will increase dramatically. The NCES *Bulletin* of September 9, 1981, states: "By 1990 older students are expected to account for 47 percent of the 12.1 million students enrolled." Soon after 1990, adult students might well be in the majority on American campuses.

ADMISSION PROSPECTS

Don't be apprehensive about the detailed admissions criteria outlined in most college catalogs: high school course prerequisites, recommendations, and college entrance examination scores. The chances are good that some of the requirements may not apply to you as an adult. Admissions officers recognize that an individual's academic record as an adolescent frequently bears little relationship to that person's academic performance as an adult. Even if your college has not formally announced special admissions criteria for adults, you may find that it provides adults with alternative means of gaining admission, and you should inquire about this possibility.

For example, the *New York Times* published an article by Harry Gersh who was admitted to Harvard as a freshman at age 63. Mr. Gersh explained, "I bothered the admissions office until they agreed to let me in." Then the *Times* provided a follow-up three years later when Mr. Gersh graduated — magna cum laude. If you are as qualified as the young graduating high school senior (and many adults are), you stand a good chance of being admitted to the college of your choice, whether it is your local college or a distant school. In fact, you should apply to more than one college if it is convenient for you to do so, perhaps two or three. Acceptance by at least one is then more likely.

THE HIGH SCHOOL DIPLOMA OR ITS EQUIVALENT

The high school diploma is the traditional basic requirement for college admission. But today you do not have to be a high school graduate in order to enroll at many colleges. You may qualify by passing a high school equivalency examination, by securing a Competency-Based or External High School Diploma, or by taking college courses to demonstrate your capacity for college-level work.

Nationally, the Tests of General Education Development (GED) are administered to allow adults to meet state requirements for high school graduation. If satisfactory scores are attained, the adult receives a certificate that is the legal equivalent of a regular high school diploma. Classes to prepare you for the GED are available during the regular school year. Details may be obtained from your community high school or your state education department.

The Competency-Based High School Diploma (CBHSD) has an instructional system, based primarily on adult performance level life skills, that is open-ended and self-paced. Each entering student goes through an assessment phase resulting in an individualized prescription for obtaining the diploma. The system is structured to allow credit for competencies the student is able to demonstrate at the time of entry, so nobody has to learn subject matter already mastered. Successful participants earn a regular diploma from a local high school. Contact the director of adult education at your local high school or your state director of adult education for the availability of this program. Additional information may be obtained from

> Jim C. Cates, Director
> APL Project
> Education Annex, S–21
> The University of Texas
> Austin, Texas 78712.

The New York State External High School Diploma was created in 1972 and currently helps adults in eight states. Adults first go through a diagnostic phase. If the results indicate that a person is not yet ready for the program, advice is given on learning resources that can be used to prepare for entry. Two types of assessment are undertaken: generalized and specialized. In generalized assessment, the adult is examined on 64 life and basic skills competencies. In individualized assessment, the adult must demonstrate an occupational skill, a special skill (for example, photography), or an advanced academic skill. For information on taking this program in Connecticut, Maryland, Massachusetts, Michigan, Montana, New York, Rhode Island, and Virginia, send a self-addressed stamped envelope to

> Dr. Kathleen Z. Porter
> Syracuse Research Corporation
> Merrill Lane
> Syracuse, New York 13210.

Several state education departments award high school equivalency diplomas to residents who complete 24 credits of college course work. Your state may have such a provision.

Even if the college you wish to attend will not grant you regular admission without a high school diploma, you might be able to enroll as a nonmatriculated (not enrolled for a degree) or "special" student and take courses for credit. As you progress, the college will assess how well you are doing, and then, if you are qualified for matriculation based on your performance, it will apply the credits toward your degree. (One note of caution: Nonmatriculated students are generally ineligible for most sources of financial aid.) If the college of your choice will not allow you to take courses without being matriculated, you might be able to take your first 24 credits at another local college to get your high school equivalency diploma, and then you can transfer the credits.

PRESENTING YOUR CREDENTIALS EFFECTIVELY

Undergraduate admission applications for most colleges are short and straightforward. Be sure to fill out the forms exactly as directed. On the form or an addendum sheet, be sure to list any significant continuing education courses you have completed, including employer and armed forces training programs. Also list any professional certifications earned such as teaching, nursing, or real estate licenses. You might also consider attaching a copy of your resume or a short autobiography accompanied by copies of awards or letters of commendation. Admissions officers usually want to know how you have spent your time since you left formal education.

If you have any doubt about the strength of your academic credentials, you might enclose an essay to demonstrate your strong motivation to pursue a college education. In the essay you could comment on your previous academic, employment, or personal experiences and the ways they relate to your current desire to attend college. Ask a friend or co-worker who writes well to critique your essay. Then have it typed and proofread.

Letters of recommendation often are not required for admission to colleges at the undergraduate level. However, if your college requires them, you should get present or past supervisors at work, or professional acquaintances, to comment on your potential for college-level work. Be sure the persons writing your references respect and like you. You should give people ample time to complete the recommendations and still meet the college deadline.

COLLEGE ENTRANCE EXAMINATIONS: SAT AND ACHIEVEMENT TESTS AND ACT

Although many colleges do not require standard admissions tests for adults, some will want to see your scores on one of the two nationally recognized college entrance examinations: the College Board's Scholastic Aptitude Test (SAT) or the American College Testing Program's examination (ACT assessment). Some colleges give applicants the option of submitting scores from either the SAT or the ACT, while others specify one test or the other. Some of the more selective schools also require College Board Achievement Tests, which measure reasoning ability and proficiency in specific subjects.

The SAT is designed to measure developed academic ability in verbal and mathematical areas. All the questions are multiple choice, and you are given 30 minutes to complete each of five sections. In addition, a half-hour Test of Standard Written English (TSWE) helps place you at the appropriate level in a freshman English course. This test does not affect your SAT score. Information and registration forms for both the SAT and College Board Achievement

Tests can be obtained from high school guidance counselors or from

The College Board
Admissions Testing Program
Box 592
Princeton, New Jersey 08541.

The ACT assessment consists of four tests of 35 to 50 minutes each. The multiple-choice questions focus on analytical and problem-solving skills and also require some general subject knowledge. ACT information and registration forms are available from high school counselors or from

ACT Registration
Box 414
Iowa City, Iowa 52234.

Can you prepare yourself to score higher on college entrance examinations? This is a hotly debated issue among agencies involved in preparing and supervising such tests. You can find preparation courses advertised in many large cities. Some people say that such courses can merely acquaint you with the test format, and that you could get similar aid at less cost if you study one of the practice books that contain sample questions. (Certainly, as a minimum preparation, you should familiarize yourself with the format and practice answering some sample questions.) The College Board offers a booklet, *Taking the SAT, A Guide for Students,* which includes sample tests and answer sheets. To get a copy, write to

The College Board
Admissions Testing Program
Box 592
Princeton, New Jersey 08541.

If you are unhappy with your scores on college entrance examinations, you may take the tests again. The

Application Checklist

	INSTITUTION 1	INSTITUTION 2	INSTITUTION 3	INSTITUTION 4
College Name	_____	_____	_____	_____
Application Fee	_____	_____	_____	_____
Admissions Deadlines:				
Priority Date	_____	_____	_____	_____
Closing Date	_____	_____	_____	_____
Early Decision Deadline	_____	_____	_____	_____
Will College Admit You Without Completing High School (yes or no)	_____	_____	_____	_____

College Board will present all scores to the college admissions office, but ACT does not. Colleges have different procedures when presented with more than one set of scores; some consider only the highest, while others may also take the lower scores into consideration.

Remember, though, that many colleges have special admissions criteria for adults. Even if the admissions policy clearly stipulates that the SAT or ACT examinations are required, you might want to request an exception. As an adult, your aptitude for college-level work can probably be determined by an evaluation of your experience and achievements.

DEADLINES IN THE ADMISSIONS CALENDAR

Timing may be important to you in gaining admission. Many colleges accept enrollments twice a year, in the fall and spring. Colleges on trimester or quarter systems often admit students three or four times a year, before the beginning of each period of instruction. Some colleges accept applications after their stated deadline. Also, a large percentage of colleges have a "rolling" admissions policy, which means that applications are considered as soon as they are received and decisions on admission are rendered soon thereafter.

You should note any admissions deadlines on the Application Checklist as soon as you decide to apply. Then use the Deadline Checklist to help you make sure that you meet all necessary deadlines. This is especially important if you want to attend a selective school, since they usually have firm deadlines. Also, you will need sufficient time to complete your application and have your transcripts and any other necessary documents mailed to the college.

Deadline Checklist

	INSTITUTION 1		INSTITUTION 2		INSTITUTION 3		INSTITUTION 4	
	Date Due	Date Sent	Date Due	Date Sent	Date Due	Date Sent	Date Due	Date Sent
Application Form	___	___	___	___	___	___	___	___
Essay	___	___	___	___	___	___	___	___
High School Completion Results:								
Transcript of High School Grades	___	___	___	___	___	___	___	___
Transcript of College Grades	___	___	___	___	___	___	___	___
GED Results	___	___	___	___	___	___	___	___
Competency-Based or External High School Diploma	___	___	___	___	___	___	___	___

Test Scores:

SAT | | | | | | | |

ACT | | | | | | | |

CLEP | | | | | | | |

Other_____ | | | | | | | |

Letters of Recommendation

1. _____ | | | | | | | |

2. _____ | | | | | | | |

3. _____ | | | | | | | |

Interview | | | | | | | |

Other_____ | | | | | | | |

Most colleges charge a nonrefundable fee for applying for admission. It can range from $10 to $25 or more. If you cannot afford this fee, and some students cannot, write to the director of admissions and ask whether or not the college will waive the fee. It is important to check this well in advance of the application deadline and put all pertinent information on the checklist.

INTERVIEWS

Interviews at many colleges are not always a part of the selection process but may be an important part of the screening process for certain adult programs. If you are asked to come for an interview, be prepared to comment on why you want to go to college and why you are interested in that particular institution. Come prepared with a list of specific questions about the programs that interest you. This will demonstrate your thoughtful concern about choosing this college and one of its programs.

FOR THOSE WHO DECIDE
AT THE LAST MINUTE

If you have missed admissions deadlines but decide at the last minute you want to go to college, you may have a "walk-on" option. It occurs during the two- or three-week period just before school opens, through registration, to just after registration. Sometimes schools discover quite late that their projections of enrollment are not being met. If you apply during this period you might be accepted.

In summary, your chances of being accepted by the college of your choice are excellent. You can compete successfully, both during the application process and later as a college student. Your careful preparation and attention to detail during the application stage will greatly enhance your chances for success.

"I'm delighted there is such a thing as credit-by-examination for people like me: when you quit a good-paying job and go back to school, you don't want to waste a minute."

Barbara Eubanks, CLEP's one millionth test candidate.

4

You Can Cut Time and Costs

CREDIT-BY-EXAMINATION

Today there are numerous opportunities for cutting the time, and thus the costs, of acquiring a college education. For example, explore the possibilities of credit-by-examination. Many colleges award credit toward degrees on the basis of the College-Level Examination Program (CLEP), which was developed by the College Board, or the College Proficiency Examinations Program (CPEP) and Regents External Degree Program of the University of the State of New York, which are administered outside of New York State by the American College Testing Program.

CLEP is a national program of credit-by-examination that enables adults to earn college credit for academic learning achieved outside the classroom. CLEP can help you gain college credit in academic areas such as English literature, American history, or college algebra. More than 35 general and subject area examinations are available, and more than 1,800 institutions in the country recognize college credit based on the results. Colleges will award credit for one- or two-semester courses based on results of examinations and will grant up to two years of college credit. Not all colleges offer credit-by-examination, and the amount of credit awarded varies from one college to another. To find out where and when you can take CLEP examinations, consult the director of admissions or the counseling department of your local college or university. Ask if counseling programs, workshops, and orientation classes are held for people interested in taking CLEP exams.

More than 25 College Proficiency Examinations are offered in New York in the arts, sciences, education, health, nursing, and criminal justice. In addition there are 25 other tests, called Regents External Degree Examinations, available in nursing, business, and foreign languages. Colleges and universities may accept results on these exams and award college credit; check with the institutions you are interested in to determine their policies. Outside of New York State this program is known as the American College Testing Program Proficiency Examination Program (ACT PEP) tests. Study guides and examination content outlines are available for these exams. See "Sources of Financial Aid Information," page 103, to learn more about this program.

If you are interested in credit-by-examination, do not overlook the possibility of using financial aid funds to cover the cost of such examinations, although those costs are not included in determining your eligibility for aid. Your employer's fringe benefit plan might also pay for examination fees, so be sure to check with the appropriate person in the personnel office of the company for which you work.

CREDIT FOR PRIOR LEARNING

A growing number of colleges offer credit for prior learning. Many adults have completed formal courses of study in military service or places of employment. Some colleges award credit for these learning experiences on the basis of recommendations by the American Council on Education and the Program on Noncollegiate Sponsored Instruction of the New York State Education Department. Another way life and work experience can qualify an individual for credits is through individual college evaluation. Usually, an institution awards these credits after it assesses a person's record of experience during which learning occurred.

The Council for the Advancement of Experiential Learning (CAEL) Learners' Services Program helps learners identify programs that award academic credit through assessment of prior learning. Call and ask for a free list of institutions in your state that offer credit for prior learning.

If you have been in military service, CAEL Learners' Services can tell you which colleges and universities accept military experience and the credit recommendations of the American Council on Education. For more information, call (301) 997-3535 weekdays from 9 a.m. to 5 p.m. Eastern time or write to

> CAEL
> Lake Front North, Suite 300
> Columbia, Maryland 21044.

What is the likelihood that you have had prior learning experiences for which you now can get college credit? A COMP/ACTIVITY Inventory, available through CAEL Learners' Services, is one method to determine in advance what credit you might expect to receive. If you complete the 54-item test and send it to CAEL offices, the Learners' Services will send you a report on receiving prior learning credit in the areas of the humanities, social sciences, life sciences, communicating, problem solving, and value-clarifying activities. CAEL also has several publications for the adult student interested in prior learning credit. Information on all of them can be found in "Sources of Financial Aid Information," page 103. Use of CAEL Learners' Services can help you effectively accelerate completion of a college degree and thus reduce the cost of your education.

EXTERNAL DEGREE PROGRAMS

These provide the opportunity for earning an undergraduate degree by taking low-cost examinations, transferring credit for courses taken previously, and pursuing independent study. No classroom attendance is required, and students from any state may enter the programs. Again, do not overlook the possibility of financial aid when seeking admission to these programs. If you qualify, it can make low-cost programs even more affordable.

NONTRADITIONAL DEGREE PROGRAMS

Many institutions have their own special nontraditional degree programs for both undergraduate and graduate students. Some can be completed entirely through part-time study. Most offer flexible time schedules and require less classroom attendance than traditional programs. There are colleges without campuses, such as Empire State College of the State University of New York, where a student works out an individualized degree program with a mentor through a series of learning contracts that contain activities such as independent study projects. Special adult degree programs in liberal studies at both the bachelor's and master's levels are offered by several colleges and universities (Goddard College, in Vermont, and the University of Oklahoma are examples). Weekend colleges within postsecondary institutions feature special credit programs (Fairleigh Dickinson University and the University of San Francisco are examples).

LESS EXPENSE

Another way of cutting educational costs is to select less expensive programs and institutions. Public colleges and universities and community colleges are generally less expensive than private or independent colleges because taxes assist in their support. But don't rule out any college because of the costs listed in its catalog. If you qualify for financial aid, the costs at private or independent colleges may turn out to be no higher than the costs at public institutions.

Of course, some of the best learning opportunities are free. Thousands of adults find do-it-yourself study extremely rewarding. Some institutions also offer free concerts, seminars, and library services. Museums, public libraries, and community organizations such as the Y's are a rich source of programs and classes, at little or no cost.

If you'd like or need some assistance from a counselor in finding the opportunities that best meet your interests, try your public library, community counseling center, local college, state educational telephone network or hotline, Educational Opportunity Center, or Talent Search project. If you have difficulty finding a counselor, see "Sources of Financial Aid Information," page 103, for some leads.

Remember that when you are going to college you are, in fact, purchasing services. Explore your options carefully and search for the best possible bargain without compromising your educational goals. You have the right as an educational consumer to be informed about alternatives available to you.

Asking the right questions of the right people at the right time is exactly what's required to come up with a sound personal financing strategy.

5

Ten Questions and Answers about Financial Aid

1 What are your chances for financial aid?

Money is available for financial aid for college-level study, but many self-supporting adults do not apply because they think that aid is only for the poor, the young, or for "straight A" students. Your chances are still good for some aid (if only a loan), even if your yearly income is about $15,000 or if you did not do well in school when you were younger. Colleges may award financial aid only to a few adult students, or on a limited or restricted basis. But don't be discouraged from applying if you really want to attend a particular institution. Aid is available whether you go to a community college, a four-year university, a vocational school, or you study on your own through correspondence or independent study courses.

2 What does financial aid consist of?

Financial aid is money to help you meet the costs of your education. It may be in the form of grants and scholarships, which do not have to be repaid and are sometimes called gift aid; loans, which generally carry a low interest rate and are repaid after you graduate or leave school; and employment, which is provided so that you can earn money to help meet your educational expenses. One type of employment is sometimes called work-study. Financial aid is available from federal and state governments, and through the financial aid offices at many colleges, universities, external degree programs, and proprietary and vocational schools. There are also many special programs that provide aid to certain groups of adults. In all cases, financial aid adds to the money you are able to spend for your education.

3 Is financial aid available for any type of learning?

Most financial aid is available only to students enrolled in degree or certificate programs. You may have difficulty finding aid for noncredit courses or credit courses that are not part of a degree program — such as those offered by most community organizations, museums, and public libraries, and by some colleges for personal development. Many aid programs have restrictions that exclude students enrolled part-time. Some programs provide aid only to undergraduates. Others provide aid to students taking postsecondary courses in vocational-technical schools.

4 What does college cost?

The first step in planning how you will pay for college is estimating your own expenses. Use the student expense budget worksheet on page 35 to calculate your own budget. To make an initial estimate, you may want to refer to the catalogs of the colleges that interest you, the financial aid materials provided by them, and *The College Cost Book*, published by the College Board, which lists expenses at 3,200 institutions. The only expenses you can be certain of are tuition and fees. Be aware of all the fees that may be charged to you: student activity, application, registration, laboratory, residence hall room-key deposit, and many more, which will vary with the institution. Other expenses such as transportation, personal items, and food may be difficult to estimate, so be careful when you add these costs to your total budget. Fees can add up and often must be paid at the beginning of each academic period.

As an adult student, you may plan to stay in your

present housing, move to a location closer to college, or live in a residence hall. Your housing decision will have a major effect on your educational costs and therefore your budget. Think about each alternative. Discuss your situation with a financial aid administrator or counselor. Frequently, the financial aid office has someone available who is responsible for and familiar with adult financial aid problems.

Remember, all your expenses for college will not be new ones. This is particularly true if you expect to live at home, wear the same clothing, and eat the same meals. In fact, you may spend less on clothing and food. Students typically dress more informally than people who work, and college cafeterias cost less than public restaurants. On the other hand, it will be best for you to overestimate expenses in order to be safe. Again, talk it over with someone in a financial aid office or ask a friend who goes to college. Do your cost estimating and budget planning carefully. Your education may depend upon it.

There are many different kinds of postsecondary educational institutions to choose from: community colleges, vocational-technical schools, public or private universities. They can be near home or far away. Costs can differ greatly from one institution to another, so make an estimate of expenses for each college you are considering.

The types of expenses you need to consider are direct educational costs (tuition, fees, books, and supplies) and living costs (room, board, commuting expenses, and personal expenses). If you have any unusual expenses, such as child care or ongoing medical needs, you should include them in your budget, too.

For example, take the cases of Andrea, Beth, and Carlos (see page 35). Andrea is a full-time student at a public community college. She sometimes stays late on campus and eats dinner as well as lunch there. She must have a babysitter for her two-year-old daughter when she is in class or the library. Beth is a half-time student at a

Student Expense Budgets

	ANDREA Full-time, 2-year public institution	BETH Half-time, 4-year public institution	CARLOS Half-time, private institution
Per Year			
1. Tuition and fees	$ 480	$ 650	$1,850
2. Books and supplies	250	250	250
3. Student's housing	Not applicable	Not applicable	Not applicable
4. Student's meals*	1,130	940	1,000
5. Personal (clothing, laundry, recreation, medical)	600	670	580
6. Transportation**	570	300	300
7. Other expenses (child care, handicap, etc.)	450 (child care)	0	300 (handicap)
8. Total budget (add 1 through 7)	$3,480	$3,040	$4,600

* *You will want to consider these expenses even if you live at home.*
** *If you are planning to live on campus, you should estimate the cost of the round trips you will make to your home. Colleges usually estimate that a student makes two or three round trips during the year. Students living at home should figure the costs of daily transportation to the college.*

public four-year college. She attends classes in the evening. Carlos is a half-time student at a private institution and attends classes in the evening. Because of a handicap, he has physical therapy expenses.

Your estimate of expenses may be higher or lower than these examples, but don't let a high estimate of expenses discourage you. High-cost institutions generally have more financial aid available to help students meet expenses.

5 How can you get aid?

Most colleges and state or other scholarship programs will ask you to complete the Financial Aid Form (FAF) of the College Scholarship Service (CSS) of the College Board or the American College Testing Program's Family Financial Statement (FFS). A copy of the FAF is in Chapter 12, "1982–83 Financial Aid Form and CSS Worksheet."

The FAF collects financial information about you and your family that institutions and programs use to determine your need for financial aid. You should check with each institution and program to make sure that you know what forms to file and when to file them. (Some colleges and programs ask students to complete institutional applications, too.) Remember, applying for admission to a college is not enough. If you think you will need financial aid, you must apply for it!

Check the deadlines for each college, state program, or other scholarship program to which you plan to apply. You should file the FAF as soon as possible after January 1 — and preferably at least four weeks before the earliest deadline you need to meet. The key is to find out *what* you have to do, *when* you have to do it, and to DO IT! Give yourself the best chance — plan ahead, apply early.

You will be asked questions about your financial situation — questions about income, assets, and family size. Your answers to these questions help the financial aid administrators at the colleges or programs to which you are applying evaluate your overall financial strength and what you can reasonably be expected to contribute toward meeting college costs.

Detailed step-by-step instructions will accompany the FAF. You will want to refer to your most recent federal income tax return if you have it. However, don't delay filing early if you haven't completed your tax return. Estimate amounts to the best of your knowledge and send corrections later, if necessary. To prevent processing delays, fill out the FAF completely. (Don't leave any items blank — if an answer is zero enter a 0). Also, keep in mind that some colleges may request a copy of your latest tax return to verify the information you reported on the FAF before they make a final aid award. The information you report is kept strictly confidential. Only those institutions and programs you designate receive a copy of your FAF.

The CSS analyzes the information you report and makes a preliminary estimate of what you could probably contribute to meeting your educational expenses. This information is printed on an FAF Need Analysis Report (FAFNAR) and is sent, along with a copy of your original FAF, to the colleges and programs you designated when you filed the form. Remember, CSS does not administer funds, but provides information and assistance to you in applying for financial aid.

And at about the same time that the FAFNAR is mailed to institutions, the CSS will send an FAF Acknowledgment to you. You should review this acknowledgment to make sure that all the institutions and agencies you are applying to have received a copy of your FAF and FAFNAR. You can also use the acknowledgment to add other institutions or agencies, including the federal programs, to your original list. The acknowledgment will also show all the information used in the analysis and will have instructions for necessary corrections.

You will eventually receive communications from the colleges, state agency, and Pell Grant program. Review all your award notices and other communications carefully, and supply additional information as requested. For most financial aid programs, you must reapply each academic year to continue receiving an award.

6 Is most financial aid based on need?

You do not have to be poor to be eligible for aid, but for most programs you do have to show financial need, which is the difference between what it costs to study and what you (and your spouse) can afford to pay toward meeting those expenses. It is important to remember that the cost of education includes all educationally related expenses, which may cover travel, extra meals away from home, and child care, as well as tuition and books. As you know, costs vary widely from institution to institution, but the amount that you are expected to pay generally does not vary. For example, if it is determined that you are able to pay $900 toward your education expenses, your financial need for aid as a part-time student at different colleges might look like this:

	COLLEGE A	COLLEGE B	COLLEGE C	COLLEGE D
Total cost	$1,200	$3,000	$5,400	$9,800
What you can pay	−900	−900	−900	−900
Your need	$ 300	$2,100	$4,500	$8,900

If you are awarded aid to cover your full need at these colleges, you would pay $900, whether you decided to go to the college with the lowest or the highest costs.

Different aid programs may have different ways of determining your financial need. You might show substantial need under one program, yet almost none under another. Explore all programs for which you might be eligible and then apply. In addition, you should note that most financial aid programs require that you make "satisfactory academic progress" in order to receive financial aid. These standards of academic performance vary from institution to institution, and generally are outlined in the college's catalog or financial aid application forms.

7 Should you borrow?

Borrow if necessary. We have become accustomed to borrowing for many things: automobiles, furniture, appliances, vacations, and more. Borrowing for an education seems to be a reasonable and sensible thing to do, especially if a college education is very important to you. An educational loan is a good source of money, but it must be repaid. If you decide to borrow, apply for a National Direct Student Loan (NDSL) through your financial aid application or a federally insured Guaranteed Student Loan (GSL) or PLUS by special application. You can get these applications at schools, state agencies, and other financial lending institutions. You can borrow under a number of loan programs, but be careful. They may all be due for repayment at the same time after you graduate or leave college, so review the repayment obligations with your financial aid counselor before you accept more than one loan. (A new program, OPTIONS, allows you to consolidate student loans received from two or more institutions under three federal programs.

See "Sources of Financial Aid Information," page 110). Local organizations and agencies may sponsor loan programs that offer better terms than commercial lenders, as may the college you are considering.

8 Is aid available for part-time students?

Generally, aid for part-time students is limited, and you must search for information on it. Most aid programs are open only to students who study at least half-time (generally six credit hours per semester or the equivalent; the exact definition may vary from school to school). Usually, part-time students who take less than six credit hours per semester, or the equivalent, are not eligible for aid.

Some federal aid programs give institutions discretion on how to allocate the funds. For example, recent changes in federal laws allow institutions to direct up to 10 percent of their funds to the Supplemental Educational Opportunity Grant Program (SEOG) and College Work-Study (CW-S) Program for students attending less than half-time (see page 52). However, there may be reductions in the size of these programs in the next few years. Check with the financial aid officer of each college you are interested in to find out if these funds are available to part-time learners.

Usually, each institution has its own restrictions or policies on awarding aid to part-time students. Many award most of their institutional aid to full-time students; some offer only loans or employment to half-time or part-time students. Some programs have minimum award requirements. In these, part-time students may show financial need and still not receive aid, because the amount of funds needed falls below a minimum level. Fortunately, other programs will provide a fixed amount of aid for any need under a minimum amount (for example, students will receive $50 if their financial need falls below the limit). Under most aid programs, the number of years you are eligible to apply for aid will increase if you study part-time (currently, you may be eligible for Pell Grants as long as you are working on your first undergraduate degree). Because policies differ, you may be turned down for aid at one college yet qualify for funds at another. Since these policies are not always stated in the college catalog, talk with the financial aid administrator at each college you are considering and find out what may be available to you.

9 What consumer rights do you have?

According to the United States Department of Education, you should ask an institution:

- What financial assistance is available, including information on all federal, state, and institutional financial aid programs.
- What the deadlines are for submitting applications for each of the financial aid programs available.
- What the cost of attending is, and what the policies are on refunds to students who drop out.
- What criteria are used to select financial aid recipients.
- How your financial need is determined. This process includes how costs for tuition and fees, room and board, travel, books and supplies, personal and miscellaneous expenses, etc., are considered in your budget.
- What resources (such as parental contribution, other financial aid, your assets, etc.) are considered in the calculation of your need.

- How much of your financial need, as determined by the institution, has been met.
- To explain the various programs in your student aid package. If you believe you have been treated unfairly, you may go through an appeal process for reconsideration of the award that was made to you.
- What portion of the financial aid you receive must be repaid, and what portion is grant aid. If the aid is a loan, you have the right to know what the interest rate is, the total amount that must be repaid, the payback procedures, the length of time you have to repay the loan, and when repayment is to begin.
- How it determines whether or not you are making satisfactory progress, and what happens if you are not.
- The name of its accrediting organizations.
- About its programs; its instructional, laboratory and other physical facilities; and its faculty.
- How and when you will receive your award(s).
- What services are available to part-time students.

10 What consumer responsibilities do you have?

According to the United States Department of Education, it is your responsibility to

- Review and consider all information about an institutution's program before you enroll.
- Pay special attention to your application for student financial aid, complete it accurately, and submit it on time to the right place. Errors can delay your receiving financial aid. Intentional misreporting of informa-

tion on application forms for federal financial aid is a violation of law and is considered a criminal offense subject to penalties under the United States Criminal Code.

- Submit all additional documentation, verification, corrections, or new information requested by either the financial aid office or the agency to which you submitted your application.
- Read and understand all forms that you are asked to sign and keep copies of them.
- Accept responsibility for all agreements you sign.
- If you have a loan, notify the lender of changes in your name, address, or school status.
- Perform in a satisfactory manner the work that is agreed on in accepting a College Work-Study award.
- Know and comply with the deadlines for application or reapplication for aid.
- Know and comply with your school's refund procedures.
- Make "satisfactory academic progress" toward the completion of your program of study.

I thought my income was too high to qualify for financial aid. I knew I couldn't afford to pay for college and support myself, but a Guaranteed Student Loan made it all possible.

6

Five Federal Student Aid Programs

Despite recent cutbacks, the federal government is still the largest single source of financial aid to students. In 1981–82, the United States Department of Education administered programs that offered more than $6 billion in aid. You may be eligible even if you do not have a high school diploma or the equivalent.

To qualify for at least some aid under one or more of the federal student aid programs, you generally must be

- Planning to study at least half-time (that is, typically a minimum of six credits per semester or the equivalent).
- Enrolled or planning to enroll in a program that leads to a degree or a certificate.
- Planning to attend an eligible educational institution or to participate in an approved external degree program (that is, approved to offer financial aid – some are not).
- A United States citizen, national, or permanent resident; or a permanent resident of commonwealth or trust territories of the United States. Or possess documentation from the United States Immigration and Naturalization Service stating that you are in the country for other than a temporary purpose.

PELL GRANTS

The largest federal government student aid program is the Pell Grant Program, formerly known as the Basic Grants Program or the Basic Educational Opportunity Grant (BEOG) Program. These grants are based on your family financial circumstances (whether you are a full-time or half-time student), how long you will be an enrolled student during a twelve-month period (July 1 through June 30 of the following year), and the cost of education at the school you plan to attend. In the academic year 1981–82, these grants for full-time study ranged from $120 to $1,670. Currently, to apply for a Pell Grant, you may submit any one of the following federally approved forms: the Financial Aid Form (FAF), the Family Financial Statement (FFS), the Application for Federal Student Aid (AFSA), the Pennsylvania Higher Education Assistance Application (PHEAA), or the Student Aid Application for California (SAAC) – the latter two only for residents of Pennsylvania or California, respectively. Once you have the forms, be sure to read the directions carefully. Federal regulations may change the application procedures. Forms are available from financial aid offices and public libraries, while the AFSA also can be obtained by writing to

Federal Student Aid
Box 84
Washington, D.C. 20044.

Contact the financial aid office at each institution you are considering to find out which of the five forms they will accept and where to send the completed forms. Of course, the most common question that prospective adult students ask is, "Am I eligible?" To help you answer that question, consult a copy of the Pell Grant Formula, available free by writing to Federal Student Aid.

The only sure way to find out if you are eligible for aid is to apply for it. Pell Grants are normally based on your income for the previous year (that is, generally the year before you actually apply). If unemployment, disability, separation, divorce, or death of a working spouse has drastically reduced your family income since you submitted your initial application, your chances for a Pell Grant are increased, and you should file a Special Condition Form. You can obtain the form from a college financial aid office or by writing to Federal Student Aid. You should apply for a Pell Grant each year that you are a student working on your first undergraduate degree.

Within six weeks of applying for a Pell Grant you

should receive a Student Aid Report (SAR), which lists your student aid index (SAI). To be eligible for a Pell Grant, your SAI must fall in the range 0–1,600. Check the information on your application for accuracy and return the SAR if there are corrections. Thousands of eligible students fail to take this simple step each year and are not awarded Pell Grants. If you have not decided where you want to study and your SAR indicates you are eligible for a Pell Grant, call or write to the financial aid office at each institution you are considering and tell them your SAI. The offices will give you an idea of what your grant would be. Your Pell Grant amount may differ from institution to institution, so it's worth checking ahead. For example, your SAI is 500. You are considering three colleges, and you will attend on a half-time basis wherever you go. The total cost of instruction for twelve months would be $1,000 at College A, $2,000 at College B, and $3,500 at College C. The financial aid offices tell you that your Pell Grant for 1981–82 would be $176 at College A, $426 at College B, and $558 at College C. Since the amount of the Pell Grant varies by attendance status (full or part-time) and total cost of instruction, do shop around by checking with each college you are considering and by obtaining the award figure.

If you are just starting a four-year undergraduate degree and intend to study on at least a half-time basis, under current law you are eligible for a Pell Grant until you have completed your first undergraduate degree. You must reapply each year and make satisfactory academic progress according to the standards required by the institution you are attending. However, since your eligibility for some forms of aid such as state grants may run out before you finish, you should explore taking CLEP or CPEP examinations (see page 26) and obtaining credit for prior learning experiences (see page 27) to get enough advanced standing to avoid this problem. Check these possibilities with the college admissions office at each institution you are considering as early as possible.

While it is possible to apply for a Pell Grant after you begin your studies, the deadline for priority consideration for other aid at most colleges is much earlier (as early as February). Therefore, apply early for all forms of aid to maximize your chances for financial assistance.

GUARANTEED STUDENT LOANS AND PLUS (ALAS) LOANS

Guaranteed Student Loans (GSL) are a major source of funds for collegiate study. These loans are primarily made by banks, savings and loan associations, and credit unions, although some colleges also are lenders. You may only borrow on a GSL up to the difference between what it costs to attend college and financial aid you have received from other sources. If you have never participated in the GSL program, the interest rate on your loan will be 9 percent (if you have an outstanding GSL at the former 7 percent interest rate, you can obtain a new loan at that figure). An origination fee of 5 percent is charged on the principal of the GSL and must be paid immediately.

Since October 1, 1981, you must show financial need to qualify for a GSL if your family's adjusted gross income for the previous year is over $30,000. The federal government generally pays the interest on GSLs for students until they begin repaying the loan and during authorized periods of deferments. A student whose family income is more than $30,000 is limited to that portion of financial need not met by other sources of aid. After October 1, 1981, all undergraduate students are limited to a yearly maximum GSL of $2,500, with a maximum of $12,500 for all years of undergraduate study. The limit for graduate students is $5,000 annually, and $25,000 for all GSLs at both the undergraduate and graduate levels. On GSLs granted since October 1,

1981, you have a grace period of six months after leaving school or attending less than half-time before you must begin paying the loan. After the grace period, you will be required to repay at least $600 a year ($50 a month).

Once you have been accepted by a college, begin looking for a lender. Finding a bank or lending institution (credit union, savings and loan association) that offers a GSL may be difficult. Unfortunately, not all lenders participate in the program, and those that do are not required to make loans to all applicants. Not all banks offer the maximum amount for which you might be eligible, and some banks offer loans only to full-time students. Try your local bank first. If you have trouble finding a lender, call the financial aid office at the institutions you are considering, or contact your state loan agency (see the listing in "Sources of Financial Aid Information," page 103) for suggestions.

The key is to start looking early. Be sure you need to borrow before applying, and then fill out your application at least eight weeks before you plan to use the money. Applications are available at banks, savings and loan associations, credit unions, financial aid offices, and state loan agencies. Send the completed application to the financial aid office of the colleges you are planning to attend; then submit the application to the lender after it is returned to you, if the college has not already done this for you. Also, check with the financial aid office to determine if institutional bills can be deferred while the loan is being processed.

PLUS, also known as ALAS loans, are auxiliary guaranteed loans that provide additional funds for meeting educational expenses. The interest rate on these loans is 14 percent. Independent students at the undergraduate level can borrow up to a maximum of $2,500 annually. The GSL undergraduate limits apply ($2,500 a year; $12,500 for entire undergraduate training). Independent students may concurrently have GSL and PLUS loans. The GSL limits apply. In other words, you cannot be given more than $2,500 a year in a combination of GSL and PLUS loans, nor more than $12,500 maximum at the undergraduate level. Graduate students may also use PLUS and can borrow as much as $3,000 a year and $15,000 maximum in addition to the GSL limits. Parents may borrow as much as $3,000 a year to a total of $15,000 for each child who is at least a half-time dependent undergraduate student. All borrowers must start repaying the loan within 60 days of receiving it. Borrowers who become students may receive a deferment while they are full-time students. However, students with deferments must pay the interest accrued while the loan repayments are delayed. It should be noted that these federal loan programs are subject to change by Congress. Financial aid offices can give you the latest facts about the programs and their current rules and regulations.

THREE FEDERAL CAMPUS-BASED PROGRAMS

Three other federal programs are called "campus-based" because the programs are administered to a large degree by each eligible institution (college, university, junior or community college, proprietary, or vocational-technical school). An institution can decide whether or not it wants to participate in the programs, and if it does, its financial aid office decides which students will get aid. All campus-based aid depends on the institution having funds of the amount and type each student is eligible to receive. Many colleges give campus-based aid only to full-time day students or evening students on a semester-by-semester basis, if enough money is available. Each institution sets its own policy for distributing financial aid. Be sure to ask each college you are considering about the policies for distributing loans, work-study, and grants; whether or not you will be able to get campus-based aid if you show enough financial need to qualify; and if the institution participates in all three programs. You may be turned down at one college and still get aid at another. Remember! The important thing is to ask.

Supplemental Educational Opportunity Grant Program (SEOG)

This program provides funds for undergraduate students. You may be able to get a SEOG as a less-than-half-time student. A college may choose to use as much as 10 percent of its SEOG funds for such students. To find out if the institutions you are considering do this, contact the financial aid officer at each school.

National Direct Student Loan Program (NDSL)

This program provides loans for students with need. You do not pay interest while you're enrolled in college, but six months after you leave college, repayment on interest and principal begins. Since October 1, 1981, the interest rate on NDSL loans is 5 percent. You may borrow up to $3,000 if you're enrolled in a vocational program or the first two years of an undergraduate degree, up to $6,000 for a bachelor's degree, and up to $12,000 for graduate and professional study. If you are a student in a graduate or professional program and you had an NDSL as an undergraduate, the maximum amount you may borrow is the difference between $12,000 and the amount of the previous loans.

College Work-Study Program (CW-S)

This program provides part-time jobs for undergraduate and graduate students who need financial aid. Generally, you will be paid by the hour based on the type of work you do, although in some circumstances you may be paid a salary. You must be paid at least the federal minimum wage. Employment may be in positions within the school or with outside employers, if they have established an arrangement for cw-s with the financial aid office. An institution may choose to spend as much as 10 percent of its cw-s funds for less-than-half-time students. Contact the financial aid office at colleges you wish to attend to determine their policies.

The best way to find out if you are eligible for campus-based aid is to apply, using one of the forms listed on page 47. Check with the financial aid office at each college you are considering to see which form you should use.

I was surprised that there were financial aid programs that helped people with particular needs. After I did some checking, I found one that worked for me.

Other Financial Aid Programs

STATE AID PROGRAMS

States are an important source of student financial aid. Nearly all sponsor their own programs. Although programs vary widely, some states:

- Award aid to students with financial need.
- Limit aid to residents studying at colleges within the state.
- Provide aid to part-time students (some offer aid to those attending less than half-time).

Be sure to explore what is available from your state each year you apply for aid since programs do change. For more information, call your state education department or higher education coordinating agency. The number is in the telephone book under the listing for state offices. Some states have a free financial aid hotline that will tell you what is available and where and how to apply. Find out if there is one in your state. A financial aid administrator in a nearby college can help you.

AID PROGRAMS SPONSORED BY COLLEGES AND UNIVERSITIES

In addition to the federal and state financial aid programs described above, most colleges offer their own scholarship, grant, loan, and student employment programs, and more of these programs are opening up to adults. The key again is to ask. To recruit adults, some colleges are offering aid to returning women, part-time students, and students not enrolled in a degree program. Financial aid may also include the following.

Deferred Tuition Programs

These programs often are available to all enrolled students. These programs allow you to spread tuition costs over several months by making a down payment of roughly one-third of tuition at registration time and paying the remainder in several monthly installments. At some institutions, these plans are called tuition installment payment plans. Deferred tuition may refer to a procedure that permits financial aid applicants to delay payment until an award is received.

Short-term Loans

These loans usually are available to all students. You can borrow amounts often ranging up to $500 to cover tuition, fees, and living expenses. Usually, the loan must be repaid by the end of the semester or quarter, but this may vary.

Emergency Loans

These loans are designed to help students through brief financial difficulties. They often range up to $100 and are usually repayable within the same semester or quarter. Some institutions may charge a fee for these services.

FOR ADULTS ONLY: SPECIAL AID PROGRAMS

There are thousands of special financial aid programs available to help specific groups of adults such as veterans, workers, the unemployed, and women. Although some of these programs consider your financial need in awarding aid, most do not. Many can be used for attendance at any college or proprietary or vocational school, or for external degree study. The number of students who actually qualify, of course, varies. Some programs serve only a handful, while others give aid to almost everyone who is eligible. These programs can help when federal, state, and college student aid programs cannot provide all the money you need. Getting special aid will not hurt your chances for other financial aid and may add enough to your resources so that you can afford the program you want. Eligibility requirements, application procedures, and deadlines are different for each program, so check carefully and look early. To help you locate programs that might offer aid to you, answer the questions in the Special Aid Program Finder on page 59 and read the chapter on Twelve Paths to Financial Aid, starting on page 61.

There are probably dozens of additional opportunities for special aid within your own community. To find them:

- Talk to college financial aid administrators.
- Read the local newspapers every day, particularly personal finance columns, and business and finance magazines (see "Sources of Financial Aid Information," page 103).
- Contact the local community organizations such as the Elks Club, American Legion, Kiwanis, Rotary Club, women's clubs, and other civic, fraternal, or religious groups.
- Contact local businesses and industries.
- Visit the local library and browse through the books on scholarships, grants, and financial aid programs. Be sure to ask the librarian for tips.
- Read the catalogs of nearby colleges.
- Listen to radio stations that broadcast personal finance information.

Special Aid Program Finder

Answer each of the following questions. If you answer no to a question, skip over that category. If you answer yes, turn to the page number listed next to the question, read about the programs to see if you might qualify, and communicate with the sources listed for more information.

	NO	YES	PAGE
1. Are you or your spouse employed or self-employed?	____	____	62
2. Are you unemployed or looking for a better job?	____	____	64
3. Are you an adult with low or limited income?	____	____	64
4. Are you a woman?	____	____	68
5. Are you a taxpayer?	____	____	69
6. Are you over age 60?	____	____	70
7. Are you Native American, black, Hispanic, or another minority?	____	____	71
8. Are you or your spouse in the armed services or a veteran?	____	____	74
9. Are you a parent?	____	____	78
10. Are you physically disabled or handicapped?	____	____	78
11. Are you or your spouse a disabled fireman, policeman, or member of a rescue squad?	____	____	79
12. Are you a member of a religious organization?	____	____	80
13. Are you looking for a career in nursing or the health professions?	____	____	80

- Ask your friends.
- See an educational broker or obtain a copy of *The Directory of Educational and Career Information Services for Adults* by sending $4 (prepaid, plus $1 for postage and handling) to

  National Center for Educational Brokering
  1211 Connecticut Avenue N.W., Suite 301
  Washington, D.C. 20036.

  This directory can also help you locate Educational Opportunity Centers and Talent Search projects.
- If you know which career field you wish to study, particularly at the graduate or professional level, a letter to its national association may uncover more sources of aid. Examples include the American Library Association, the Council on Social Work Education, the American Bar Association, and the Society of Women Engineers. These are listed in the United States Department of Labor's *Occupational Outlook Handbook* and in various directories of associations, available at most schools and in public libraries.

In summary, you probably live in a state that awards financial aid to qualified undergraduate students. If you demonstrate a need, your chances for receiving an award are good. And if you prove a need for still more money, the colleges or universities to which you apply will probably offer some form of additional financial aid. However, you are going to have to work harder than you would have had to in recent years, particularly in locating and obtaining special aid programs. The programs certainly do exist, but more students than ever before will be seeking funds from these sources.

"Only 5 percent of those who are eligible for employer training tuition reimbursement benefits take advantage of them."

Norman Kurland
Director, Adult Learning Services
New York State Education Department

8

Twelve Paths to Financial Aid

1 The Benefits of Working

If you are currently employed, ask the personnel office at your company or your supervisor if your employee fringe benefit package includes money for education or training. The scope of tuition aid programs is often broader than that of federal and state student aid programs, making employer tuition aid a valuable source of aid for many adults who could not meet the cost of education without some financial assistance. Employers have more than $10 billion available in educational funds each year, but only a small fraction of this money is used. Educational benefits should be thought of as part of your salary. If you are not using them, you are not receiving all of the compensation you have earned and to which you are entitled.

According to the National Institute on Work and Learning (NIWL), there are four major categories of tuition assistance, none mutually exclusive:

● *tuition reimbursement or advancement plans,* which pay all or part of tuition and related costs for enrollment in schools and colleges;
● *educational leave and leave of absence plans,* granted to employees for educational purposes for a specified period during working hours or for an extended period of time;
● *scholarships and educational loans,* with which an employer lends money or provides grants of money to qualified employees for education and training on a full or partial basis; and
● *training fund plans,* in which an employer contributes a fixed amount per employee to a central fund to finance education and training.

Company policies vary widely in the type of education that is covered (job training or retraining, college education, etc.) and the type of aid available (loans, grants, tuition refund). Many companies will pay for noncredit courses and do not require the student to enroll in a degree program or stipulate how much study should be undertaken. Because the majority of companies reimburse you only *after* you have successfully completed the course work, you may want to look into a loan to pay initial tuition costs. Guaranteed Student Loans or short-term loans offered by many colleges might be especially helpful.

Any training you have already received on the job may make you eligible for college credit if you decide to seek a degree at a postsecondary institution. Ask in the personnel office at your place of employment if in-house training programs have been examined for recommendations on college credit by the American Council on Education.

If your spouse is employed, you may be able to pay for your education through his or her fringe benefit plan, a source that should not be overlooked.

If you would like to alternate between work and study, look into a cooperative education program at a nearby college. Programs vary, so it is important to discuss specific details at each college you are considering. In some instances, you can build upon your present job to get credits. Some programs let you alternate between part-time work and part-time study. If you are interested and would like to find out which institutions participate and the specifics of each program, write to

The National Commission for Cooperative Education
360 Huntington Avenue
Boston, Massachusetts 02115.

Ask for a free copy of *Undergraduate Programs of Cooperative Education in the United States and Canada.*
If you own a small business and would like additional

training to help you run your business more effectively, the local office of the federal Small Business Administration offers free seminars, courses, and technical assistance that may help you. The number is in the telephone book under "United States Government."

2 Are You Unemployed? Do You Have Low Income and Want a Better Job?

Recent actions by the United States Congress have limited aid opportunities, but not totally eliminated them.

If you are unemployed or have low income and want a better job, look into education training under the Comprehensive Employment and Training Act (CETA). Generally, programs are skills oriented and full time, although some are open to part-time students. Job counseling may also be available. Public service employment programs have been eliminated from this law. Check with your county manpower training unit for details.

If you are unemployed, you may be able to receive unemployment benefits for several months and pursue your education or vocational training at the same time if your education is approved by the state, is job related, and will lead to potential employment. For more information, contact your state unemployment insurance office. The number is in the telephone book under the listing for state offices.

If you are an unemployed mother with low income, look into the Work Incentive Program (WIN). Through WIN you may be able to receive funds for your tuition and some support for living expenses, commuting, and lunches. You must be recommended by a social service caseworker to qualify. For more information, contact your state department of social services or state employment or job service.

If you have limited income, do not overlook food stamps, special educational opportunity programs, Aid to Families with Dependent Children, and low-rent housing assistance. While these programs are still federally funded, eligibility requirements have been tightened and individual benefits reduced in recent years.

The Food Stamp Program helps low-income households buy the food needed for good health. Food stamps are coupons that are used like money to purchase food in grocery stores. Once you are determined eligible, you are certified to obtain food stamps each month at no cost. You can qualify for food stamps as a student if you meet the regular eligibility rules plus special requirements if you are attending an institution of higher education.

The Food Stamp Program has established eligibility rules in several areas: work, income, residence, resources, citizenship, and household composition. There may be exceptions in certain cases. Able-bodied people between the ages of 18 and 60 must register for work, search for a job, and accept any suitable offer. Students enrolled at least half-time in a recognized school, training program, or post-secondary institution are exempt from registering for full-time employment during the school year.

Students in institutions of higher education must meet one of four eligibility requirements in order to participate in the Food Stamp Program:

- Be a paid employee for a minimum of 20 hours a week, or if self-employed, be employed for a minimum of 20 hours a week and receive weekly earnings at least equal to the minimum wage.
- Provide more than half support to a dependent or be the spouse of an individual providing more than half support.

● Participate in a federally financed Work-Study program.
● Be enrolled in the institution as a result of participation in the Work-Incentive Program.

A household eligible to receive food stamps cannot have countable resources greater than $1,500 unless the household consists of two or more persons, one of whom is at least 60 years of age. In this case, the household may have resources of $3,000. Countable resources include cash, savings, and checking accounts; stocks and bonds; and land and buildings, other than the home, not used to produce income. Some resources that are not considered countable are the home, licensed vehicles used to produce income, life insurance policies, household goods, and personal belongings.

To be eligible for food stamps, your household's gross income must fall within 130 percent of the federal poverty guidelines for that size of household. Changes in the cost of living are reflected in periodic adjustments to these levels. Included in the calculation of income are wages; gross earnings for self-employment minus costs; public assistance; alimony received; and scholarships, education grants, fellowships, or veterans' education benefits that are not used to pay tuition and mandatory fees.

Other types of income are not counted for food stamp eligibility, including portions of education loans, grants, scholarships, and veterans' benefits used for tuition and mandatory fees; loans (except deferred repayment loans for nonmandatory education expenses); and certain kinds of income excluded by law.

The Food Stamp Program requires you to file an application and to be interviewed by a food stamp worker. You must also supply documents and information to verify your eligibility for the program. If you are declared eligible, you will be certified to receive food stamps for a specified period of time, depending on the stability of circumstances in the household, but for no longer than 12 months. At the end of the certification period, you must reapply. If your circumstances change during this certification period, you must notify the Food Stamp Program within 10 days of the date of change.

Another source of public assistance that may be available for adult students is Aid to Families with Dependent Children (AFDC or ADC), which goes to families with minor children without adequate means of support because of the absence, death, or incapacity of a parent. The amount of assistance provided to the family depends on the size of the family and on whether or not income or resources are available for support. Monthly allowances are established for all needs of the family except rent and heat, and an additional amount is allowed for those two items.

Participants in AFDC or ADC who are employable are required to accept job referrals and reasonable employment or to participate in job training. Contact your local department of social services for further information.

Special educational opportunity programs for low-income students also may be available at local colleges, universities, and vocational-technical schools. Programs provide financial aid, counseling, tutoring, and lots of individual help. For further information, contact the financial aid office at each college you are considering. The local educational opportunity center or Talent Search project in your community also may have special programs and services. See "Sources of Financial Aid Information," page 103, to locate these programs.

Low-rent housing through the United States Department of Housing and Urban Development (HUD) may enable you to minimize your living expenses. Call the local office of HUD and ask someone in the housing management division for a list of subsidized projects or rental units in your area and the eligibility requirements. The number is in the telephone book under "United States Government."

3 Aid for Women

If you are thinking of joining the thousands of adult women returning to college, you may be eligible for aid designed just for women. Many colleges offer special aid programs for returning women. National women's organizations are another source you should explore. One of the best places to start is Catalyst, a national nonprofit organization working to expand career and family options for women. The New York City office of Catalyst (14 East 60th Street, New York, New York 10022) has a library information service available to the public and publishes career guidance materials. Catalyst will send a free list of the more than 200 career resource centers affiliated with it.

There are two excellent sources of national aid programs available to women. The 1981 edition of *Financial Aid: A Partial List of Resources for Women* is available by sending a check for $2.50 (payable to AAC/PSEW) to

Project on the Status and Education of Women
Association of American Colleges
1818 R Street, NW
Washington, D.C. 20009.

A free pamphlet, *Educational Financial Aid Sources for Women,* by the Clairol Loving Care Scholarship Program, can be obtained by sending a stamped self-addressed business-sized envelope to

Clairol Pamphlet
Box 14680
Baltimore, Maryland 21268.

Local chapters of national women's organizations, such as the American Association of University Women, the American Business Women's Association, the Business and Professional Women's Foundation, and others, may also offer awards or scholarships for the education of women in their local communities. Check with your local library, chamber of commerce, or similar organizations for more information. One good place to start is the *Selected List of Postsecondary Education Opportunities for Minorities and Women.* The book may be in the local library or can be purchased for $6.00 by including the stock number 065–000–00118–7 and writing to

U.S. Superintendent of Documents
U.S. Government Printing Office
Washington, D.C. 20402.

4 Tax Breaks

If you pay income taxes, you may be overlooking a valuable source of educational aid. At present, the federal government offers two tax advantages to adult college students. The first is a tax deduction for education used to maintain or improve skills needed in your current job. This may be a refresher course, a degree program, or a course to help you keep up with the latest changes in your area of work. The education does not have to be required by your employer, but if the courses qualify you for a new trade or business, the deduction will not be allowed. You must itemize deductions to benefit. However, travel from your job to school in the same day may be deducted, even if you do not itemize. For further information, contact the Internal Revenue Service through the number or address listed in the telephone book under "United States Government," and ask for Pamphlet 508.

The second deduction covers child-care costs. If you are a full-time student, are married to a working spouse, and have children under the age of 15, you may deduct babysitting, nursery school, or day-care expenses from your income tax. The cost of caring for a disabled spouse

or parent is also deductible. Beginning in 1982 you may be
able to reduce your tax liability for any year up to a maximum of $720 for one dependent, or $1,440 for the care of
two or more people. For more information, ask the Internal
Revenue Service for Pamphlet 503.

Many states also provide some type of tax benefit for
education. It may be an educational trust fund, where you
can put aside a certain amount in the bank each year for
your future education, and not pay taxes on the money
until you actually use it. Or it might be a tax deduction or
tax credit for tuition or child-care costs. Often you do not
have to enter a degree program to qualify, and in many
states you may be able to study part-time. Not all benefits
are available to adults, but this is changing. Check with
your state department of taxation each year for the most
up-to-date information. The number is in the telephone
book under the name of your state.

5 A Special Bargain if You Are Age 60 or Over

Thousands of older Americans are taking college
courses and paying no tuition. Many states have legislation
providing either free or greatly reduced tuition to adults
60 years of age and over who take courses at public colleges or universities. Many private colleges and colleges in
states without such legislation offer similar opportunities.

The Institute of Lifetime Learning of the National Retired Teachers Association–American Association of Retired Persons (NRTA–AARP) recently found that about
1,200 institutions of higher education are now offering free
or reduced tuition benefits. You can obtain a listing of such
schools by state (four states per request). An excellent

guide to these learning resources is *Learning Opportunities for Older Persons,* which is also published by the Institute of Lifetime Learning. A single copy is available free. For both materials write to

> The Institute of Lifetime Learning, NRTA–AARP
> 1909 K Street, NW
> Washington, D.C. 20049.

In addition, most colleges offer a number of specially priced programs designed specifically for older adults. For further information, check the local newspapers, inquire at the local library, or call your state's office on aging. The number is in the telephone book under the name of your state.

6 Aid for Minority Students

There are hundreds of programs especially designed to help minority students. One of the best places to start looking is the *Selected List of Postsecondary Education Opportunities for Minorities and Women.* (See page 113 for ordering information.)

Another excellent resource is *Minority Organizations: A National Directory,* particularly since it has an index of organizations that provide financial aid information or scholarships. Again, check for the book in your public library or purchase it for $16.00 from

> Garrett Park Press
> Garrett Park, Maryland 20896.

You may also want to contact one of these referral agencies for further information on scholarships and grants for minority students:

Asian/Pacific Americans Concern Staff
U.S. Department of Education
400 Maryland Avenue, S.W.
Washington, D.C. 20202

This agency mails, upon request, scholarship information to people of Asian/Pacific American descent.

Aspira of America
205 Lexington Avenue
New York, New York 10016

Aspira offers free preliminary counseling, college referral, and scholarship and loan information to Puerto Rican students, as well as counseling for these students after they are in college. Aspira has offices in Miami, Florida; Chicago, Illinois; Newark, New Jersey; New York, New York; Philadelphia, Pennsylvania; and Rio Piedras, Puerto Rico.

Japanese American Citizens League
1765 Sutter Street
San Francisco, California 94115

The Japanese American Citizens' League has several scholarships available to its members. They include freshman awards, undergraduate awards, graduate scholarships in both the arts and the professions (for example, law), and a special awards program. The organization has chapters in 110 cities and regional offices in Fresno, California; Los Angeles, California; Washington, D.C.; Chicago, Illinois; and Seattle, Washington.

League of United Latin American Citizens (LULAC)
National Education Service Centers, Inc.
Suite 716, 400 First Street, N.W.
Washington, D.C. 20001

The National Education Service Centers division of LULAC will provide educational counseling for low-income students and has a scholarship fund for students of Mexican, Puerto Rican, Cuban, or other Hispanic origin. LULAC has branch offices in Pomona, California; San Francisco, California; Colorado Springs, Colorado; Chicago, Illinois; Topeka, Kansas; Miami, Florida; Albuquerque, New Mexico; and Philadelphia, Pennsylvania.

National Council of La Raza
c/o Guadalupe Saavedra
Vice President for Special and International Projects
or Maria Moninuevo
Office of Special Projects
Suite 200, 1725 Eye Street, N. W.
Washington, D.C. 20006

The National Council of La Raza informs American citizens of Hispanic descent about financial aid sources and has regional offices in San Francisco, California; Chicago, Illinois; Dallas, Texas; and McAllen, Texas.

National Scholarship Service and Fund for Negro
    Students (NSSFNS)
562 Third Street
Brooklyn, New York 11215

NSSFNS is an agency that counsels all minority students. It has a free college advisory and referral service that gives students the names of institutions where they are most likely to obtain admission and financial aid. Other offices are located in Atlanta, Georgia; Jamaica, New York; and Philadelphia, Pennsylvania.

Office of Indian Education Programs and Bureau of
    Indian Affairs
18 and C Streets, N.W.
Washington, D.C. 20245

The federal Bureau of Indian Affairs (BIA) provides scholarship and loan information to Native Americans. Contact your home agency of BIA or your tribe for an application packet. Native Americans may find their own tribes a good source of aid. Tribal financial opportunities may provide nearly full financial support for college-related costs as well as money for clothing and incidentals.

7 The Military Connection

There are several ways that you can become eligible for the extensive and varied educational programs available through the military.

If you are interested in becoming an officer in the armed forces, the Reserve Officer Training Corps (ROTC) has Army, Navy, Marine, and Air Force ROTC units at public and private colleges and universities throughout the country. If you are between the ages of 17 and 25, you may be able to qualify for a scholarship to cover tuition and fees, books, and a monthly nontaxable allowance of $100. Two-, three-, and four-year scholarships may be available. You may be able to obtain a scholarship even if you are already enlisted. Further information can be obtained from the guidance office of a high school, the recruiting offices of each service, and the ROTC department at a participating college. Information is also available by writing to

> Army ROTC Scholarships (for enlisted personnel only)
> Fort Monroe, Virginia 23651

> Army ROTC Scholarships
> Box 12703
> Philadelphia, Pennsylvania 19134

> Navy Opportunity Information Center
> Box 2000
> Pelham Manor, New York 10803
> (For information on two-year program for junior and
>   senior years of college)

Air Force ROTC Advisory Service
Maxwell Air Force Base
Montgomery, Alabama 36112

Active duty in the armed services opens educational opportunities. Each service permits you to take off-duty course work and pays for 75 percent or more of tuition and fees. Special programs of this type are the Servicemen's Opportunity College (Army), the Campus Program (Navy), and the Community College of the Air Force. For complete information on the many different educational programs available to members of the armed forces on active service, contact the nearest Army, Navy, Marine, or Air Force recruiting office listed in the telephone book under United States Government.

There is also the Defense Activity for Non-Traditional Education Support (DANTES), a testing and educational services program. You may contact the nearest base education office for further details, or for information about the full range of programs you can write to

DANTES
Pensacola, Florida 32509.

Many states have educational incentives if you serve in the National Guard, and educational provisions also exist for being in a reserve unit. You can obtain information on these programs by contacting the nearest recruiting offices of the armed forces.

You are eligible for veterans' education benefits under the GI Bill if you

- Served at least 181 days of continuous active duty with any part of it after January 31, 1955, and before January 1, 1977, and you were released from active service under conditions other than dishonorable.
- Did not serve the required time because of a service-connected disability.

● Were enlisted in or assigned to a reserve unit prior to January 1, 1977, but served on active duty for at least 181 days beginning within 12 months after January 1, 1977, as a result of this enlistment or assignment.

How long you can receive GI Bill benefits depends on the number of months of active duty you served. An eligible veteran with 18 or more continuous months of active duty is entitled to receive 45 months of full-time education benefits or the equivalent in part-time benefits. Full-time enrollment is defined as 14 semester hours unless the institution certifies to the Veterans Administration that 12 hours is considered full time. One and one-half months of full-time benefits or the part-time equivalent for each month of active duty are provided to eligible veterans who have served on active duty for fewer than 18 months. If you are completing the requirements for a high school diploma or equivalency certificate or taking refresher courses prior to enrollment in a postsecondary education or training program, the basic entitlement is not charged. Eligibility will cease if you do not take advantage of these benefits within 10 years of your release from active duty or by December 31, 1989, whichever is earlier.

Institutions where you can use your GI Bill benefits include public or private elementary and secondary schools; vocational, correspondence, or business schools; colleges and universities; professional, scientific, or technical institutions; and apprenticeship programs. If you decide that you must change your program of study, you may do so once without jeopardizing your benefits. The Veterans Administration may approve additional changes.

If your GI Bill benefits have expired and you have education benefits remaining, the Veterans Administration may provide you with interest-bearing loans.

Under the Post-Vietnam Veterans' Educational Assistance program, persons entering the service after December 31, 1976, who were released under conditions other than dishonorable are eligible for matching funds from the Veterans Administration at a rate of $2 for each $1 contributed by the veteran while in the service. The Department of Defense may contribute an additional amount. The veteran's contributions are limited to a total of $2,700. Matching funds are provided by the Veterans Administration until 10 years after the date of last release or discharge from active duty after January 1, 1977. Entitlement is limited to 36 months or the number of months the veteran contributed to the program, whichever is less.

If you are a spouse, a daughter, or a son of a veteran who is completely disabled, the Veterans Administration will help cover the costs of your education. These benefits also apply to families of veterans who have died as a result of service or who have been missing in action or captured in the line of duty for more than 90 days. Generally, children of eligible veterans receive monthly payments for these benefits between the ages of 18 and 26.

You can get information and counseling on all programs for veterans from a college office of veterans affairs, or the Veterans Administration regional office nearest you (under United States Government in the telephone book). Or you may send $2.50 for the *Federal Benefits for Veterans and Dependents IS-1 Fact Sheet* to

U.S. Superintendent of Documents
U.S. Government Printing Office
Washington, D.C. 20402

Your military connection can provide you with more than direct financial assistance for current learning opportunities. Training in the armed forces may make you eligible for credit for prior learning. Colleges and universities use the *Guide to the Evaluation of Educational Experiences in the Armed Services* from the American Council on Education (see "Sources of Financial Aid Information," page 103) to grant these credits for prior learning and for the Army Military Occupational Specialties (enlisted and warrant officer MOSs) and Navy ratings. To receive these credits you must ask the institution you wish to attend to review your military experience. To start this review persons to be contacted include the registrar, the admissions counselor, and the veterans adviser. To find out which colleges near you will accept military experience and the credit recommendations of the American Council on Education, call CAEL Learners Services weekdays, 9 a.m.–5 p.m., Eastern time, at (301) 997-3535.

8 How to Meet Child-Care and Related Costs

Ask about child-care services at each college you are considering. Some colleges now provide child-care services free of charge. Many keep a list of local day-care centers in your area. If you are studying full time, your child-care costs may be tax deductible (see page 69).

If you have low income or if you or your spouse is unemployed, check the following programs to assist with child-care costs: Aid to Families with Dependent Children, Work Incentive Program (see page 64), and unemployment insurance. For information, contact your state department of social services or regional office of the United States Department of Labor (under United States Government in your telephone directory).

9 Help for the Disabled and the Handicapped

A number of state agencies offer financial aid programs to students suffering from a variety of handicaps. The amount of aid varies from state to state, and most aid must be used for education or training that will lead to a job. In many instances, aid will help cover the costs of books, supplies, living expenses, and transportation. Special equipment such as a tape recorder or a Braille transcriber may also be available free of charge. If you are seriously handicapped, funds may be used to pay a tutor, a driver, or an aide. Having the cost of any one of these services supplied could greatly reduce the extra expenses you may have and may make it possible for you to get the education you want. Remember to apply to the institutions you are thinking of attending and be sure to indicate your disability or handicap in your financial aid application. Expanded opportunities may be found in the College Work-Study Program, since financial aid officers can develop jobs specifically for handicapped students. For more information, call your state department of vocational rehabilitation, which is listed in the telephone book under the name of your state.

HEATH (Higher Education and the Handicapped), a project of the American Council on Education, responds to requests for information on higher education for the handicapped and distributes a free newsletter, *Information from HEATH/Closer Look Resource Center,* three times a year. Both voice and teletypewriter communication are available by calling (202) 833-4707, 9 a.m.–5 p.m., Eastern time, weekdays. You can also write to

HEATH
Box 1492
Washington, D.C. 20013.

10 Aid for Public Servants

A few states offer aid for the education of disabled law enforcement personnel, firemen, rescue squad workers, correction officers, or their dependents, including spouses. For more information, write your state education department or higher education coordinating agency.

11 Financial Aid from Religious Organizations

Most organized religions provide some educational assistance for their members through the synod, council, diocese, local congregation, or through affiliated federations and foundations. Call your local church or synagogue for more information.

12 Financial Aid for Nursing or the Health Professions

The Scholarship Program for First-Year Students of Exceptional Need

This program is available for people pursuing a career in medicine, osteopathy, dentistry, optometry, pharmacy, podiatry, or veterinary medicine. There are three requirements for receiving these scholarships: you must be a citizen or national of the United States or a lawful permanent resident of the United States, Puerto Rico, the Virgin Islands, Guam, the Trust Territory of the Pacific Islands or the Northern Mariana Islands; you must be accepted or enrolled as a full-time student in the first year of study in a health professions school; and you are determined to be in "exceptional financial need." The scholarship covers the

Financial Aid for Nursing or the Health Professions

PROGRAM	FOR INFORMATION CONTACT
Scholarship Program for First-Year Students of Exceptional Need	U.S. Department of Health and Human Services Public Health Service, Health Services Administration Bureau of Health Personnel Development and Service, Student and Institutional Assistance Branch 5600 Fishers Lane, Parklawn Building Rockville, Maryland 20857
National Health Service Corps Scholarship Program	National Health Service Corps Scholarship Program 3700 East West Highway Hyattsville, Maryland 20782
Nursing Student Loan Program	Health Services Administration Bureau of Health Personnel Development and Service Division of Student Services Parklawn Building, Room 8A–33 5600 Fishers Lane Rockville, Maryland 20857
Health Professions Student Loan Program	U.S. Department of Health and Student Services Public Health Service, Health Services Administration Bureau of Health Personnel Development and Service, Student and Institutional Assistance Branch Parklawn Building, Room 9A–25 5600 Fishers Lane Rockville, Maryland 20857
Health Assistance Loan Program (HEAL)	HEAL Branch 5600 Fishers Lane Parklawn Building, Room 9A-16 Rockville, Maryland 20857

cost of tuition and other reasonable educational expenses including fees, books, and laboratory expenses plus a monthly stipend for 12 consecutive months. Information and application forms for this program should be obtained at the financial aid office of the institution you wish to attend.

The National Health Service Corps Scholarship Program

This program provides a limited number of scholarships to students intending to serve in a federally designated health-manpower shortage area. Eligible fields of study include medicine, osteopathy, and dentistry. The scholarships require a year's service at a site designated by the National Health Service Corps for each year a scholarship is received, although the minimum service obligation is two years. The scholarships provide tuition, fees, reasonable education costs, and a monthly stipend. No first-time awards are scheduled for the 1982–83 school year, although that situation may change.

The Nursing Student Loan Program

This program is for people wishing to enroll half-time or full-time in a program leading to a diploma, associate degree, bachelor's degree, or graduate degree in nursing. To apply you must be a citizen, national, or permanent resident of the United States, or have personal plans to become a permanent resident. The borrowing limit is $2,500 for an academic year, and the total cannot exceed $10,000. Repayment of these loans begins nine months after leaving school at an interest rate of 6 percent. You have 10 years to repay. Deferments for a maximum of three years are possible for active duty in a uniformed service (the Public Health Service or the armed services) or for volunteer work with the Peace Corps. Full-time attendance in advanced professional training in nursing qualifies a person for a deferment of repayment for up to five years. Interest on your loan does not accrue during periods of deferment. Repayment of part of the loan is possible if you elect to serve as a full-time registered nurse in a federally designated health-manpower shortage area. For example, if you serve two continuous years in a health-manpower shortage area, the government will pay 60 percent of the unpaid balance of the loan. For three years of service, the government will pay 85 percent of the unpaid balance. Repayment requests go directly to the Division of Student Services (see address table, page 81). Information and application forms for the program should be obtained at the financial aid office of the institution you wish to attend.

The Health Professions Student Loan Program

This program is for full-time students·in programs required for becoming a physician, dentist, osteopath, optometrist, pharmacist, podiatrist, or veterinarian. You are eligible if you are a citizen or national of the United States, or have such immigration status and personal plans to indicate that you intend to become a permanent resident; if you are enrolled or accepted as a full-time student in an appropriate program; and in need of the loan (students in medicine and osteopathy must show exceptional financial need). You may borrow the cost of tuition plus $2,500 or the amount of your financial need, whichever amount is the lesser, for each school year. Currently the interest rate is 9 percent. Loans are repayable over a 10-year period beginning one year after completing or ceasing to pursue full-time study. Interest begins to accrue when the loan becomes repayable. Repayments are in equal or graduated installments based on your request when you leave full-time study. Provisions allow you to defer payments for active duty in a uniformed service, as a volunteer under the Peace Corps Act, or while pursuing advanced professional training. Interest does not accrue during periods of deferment. If you practice in a health-manpower shortage area for two or more years, 60 percent of the outstanding principal and interest may be repaid by the federal government, and an additional 25 percent may be repaid for a third year, subject to the availability of funding. Under certain circumstances your loans may be repaid, even if you did not complete your studies. Information and application forms for the program should be obtained at the financial aid office of the institution you wish to attend.

Health Education Assistance Loan Program (HEAL)

Full-time students enrolled in certain health profession programs can obtain federally insured loans for their educational expenses. Eligible programs include medicine, osteopathy, dentistry, veterinary medicine, optometry, podiatry, public health, pharmacy, chiropractic medicine, graduate health administration, and clinical psychology. Medical, dental, osteopathic, veterinary medicine, optometry, or podiatry students may borrow up to $20,000 a year, not to exceed $80,000 total for loans during all years; all other eligible students may obtain loans of $12,500 per year to an aggregate of $50,000. The interest rate is pegged to the interest rate on 91-day Treasury Bills sold at auction plus three and one-half percent, rounded to the next higher one-eighth of one percent. Repayment does not begin until nine months after the student leaves school. There are certain provisions for deferment and, in some instances, for federal repayment of portions of the loan. In general, 25 years are allowed for repayment of the loan. HEAL cannot be used for study at foreign medical schools. For more information, contact the financial aid office of the institution you wish to attend.

*The first time I applied for financial aid,
I didn't organize the information and I
missed some deadlines. When I applied
the next year, I made sure I was ready.*

9

*Organizing
Your
Financial
Aid
Plan*

This section will guide you step by step through the process of searching and applying for financial aid. Although there is no guarantee that you will receive aid, setting up a financial aid plan will save time and make your search much easier. Your plan should begin once you have decided that you want to study and have some ideas about what you would like to study. At this point, you do not have to know where you will attend or whether you will be a part-time or full-time student. Even if you are already a student, it is not too late to develop a financial aid plan. Start your plan by following the Financial Aid Checklist on page 87. Look up any words you do not understand in the "Key to Financial Aid Language," page 129.

Searching for aid is important. Not all aid programs are open to adult or part-time students. Some colleges give most of their aid to dependent full-time students, but others have started their own special aid programs specifically to serve adults. The Comparison Guide on page 92 helps you keep track of what is available at different institutions and what questions you should ask a financial aid office.

Deadlines for financial aid applications are also very important and sometimes very strict. Each college has its own deadlines for admission and financial aid applications. Many have two financial aid deadlines: an early, "preferred" deadline that gives an applicant the best chance for getting aid and a final deadline after which no applications are accepted. Ask about these deadlines early. Use the Financial Aid Calendar on page 98 to keep track of deadlines and critical dates. Write down all deadlines on the calendar — and meet them.

Your education is one of the largest investments you will ever make, so look at the real price tag. If you qualify for financial aid, the actual cost of your education can be substantially lower than the costs given in an institution's catalog. Do not settle for a less desirable education program simply because you are offered financial aid. After all, the purpose of financial aid is to place your educational goals within your reach.

Financial Aid Checklist

STEPS TO TAKE	WHEN TO TAKE THEM
1. Take the time to read this book. If you have any questions, write them down so that you can ask a counselor or college financial aid administrator.	Start right now. The earlier you start, the better are your chances of getting all the aid that is available to you.
2. Send for any information on financial aid you think might be helpful. If it seems to meet your needs, find out more about it and apply.	As early as possible.
3. Search for special sources of aid. Start with the Special Aid Program Finder on page 59 and keep looking. Mark any application deadlines on the Financial Aid Calendar on page 98.	A year in advance is not too early.
4. Ask for the free information on federal student aid programs. See a community counselor, call a nearby college financial aid office, or write to Federal Student Aid, Box 84, Washington, D.C. 20044.	After January 1 of the year you wish to apply. Programs and program eligibility rules change, so check again around the time you plan to study.
5. Find out which state student aid programs are available in your state, how to apply, and who is eligible. Ask your counselor, call a nearby college financial aid office, or contact your state higher education coordinating agency or education department.	As early as you can. Write down any deadlines on your aid calendar.

STEPS TO TAKE	WHEN TO TAKE THEM

6. Prepare an estimate of your financial need. To do this:
a. Secure your free copy of *Meeting College Costs* from counselors. This will give you an idea of the amount you may be expected to pay before you can get federal campus-based aid and state student aid.
b. Order your free copy of the Pell Grant Formula by writing to Federal Student Aid, Box 84, Washington, D.C. 20044.

After January 1 of the year you wish to apply.

7. Call or write to the institutions where you would like to study, and ask for financial aid information. In addition to inquiring about aid programs, be sure to find out in each case what is used as an estimated student budget to establish aid. Study the information using the Comparison Guide on page 92.

Five or six months before you would like to begin to study or before the academic term starts at the institution of your choice. If you are studying now, you should look into the possibility of financial aid to help continue your studies.

8. Obtain financial aid applications from all colleges you are considering. Complete and return all required forms to appropriate places. If you need help in doing so, see a college counselor.

Any time after January 1 of the year for which you are applying, but at least two months before the deadline at each institution you are considering. Mark these dates down on your calendar.

9. Plan a time when you are able to spend several hours on your applications. Get a pencil, pen, and scratch paper; then sit down with a copy of your most recent federal income tax return and complete the applications.

STEPS TO TAKE	**WHEN TO TAKE THEM**
10. Mail the applications. Do not apply for a GSL or other loans at this point, because if you apply for and receive a loan before you apply for other aid, the amount of aid that you could receive from other sources might be reduced. Maintain a record of the forms completed, to whom sent, and the mailing date. It is best to keep copies of all the forms that you send.	
11. You should receive a Student Aid Report for the Pell Grant approximately six weeks after you mail your application. Mark this date on your aid calendar. If you do not receive the SAR within that time, write to Federal Student Aid Programs, Box 92505, Los Angeles, California 90009.	
12. Use your SAR to search for aid.	
13. Send a photocopy of the SAR to each institution you would like to attend. If you are considering more than one institution, make photocopies of the SAR.	As soon as you receive the SAR.
14. Each financial aid office will send an award or rejection notice after all required application forms and materials have been received.	Find out what month each institution will send out notices. Mark those dates on your calendar.

STEPS TO TAKE	WHEN TO TAKE THEM
15. Once you receive an award notice, make an assessment. Use the Comparison Guide to compare offers. Look at the deadline date when you must accept or reject the offer and mark it on your calendar.	As soon as possible after you receive the award notices, but before the deadline by which you must either accept or reject the award.
16. Now is the time for a final decision. Weigh all factors, including cost. Accept one offer and reject all others — and respond to each institution by the deadline. Now is the time to consider a loan. You may have to check with several lenders in order to get a loan. Look into GSL and PLUS/ALAS.	At least 10 weeks before your semester or quarter begins.
17. Take a well-deserved break.	
18. Reapply next year. Remember, the eligibility rules and your financial circumstances change, so apply again, even if you did not get aid this year.	

SOME HINTS

Don't be discouraged. There are a lot of forms and applications to fill out, but if you need money for your education, it will be well worth your time to apply. Read everything through at least once and learn the ins and outs of the programs before starting to fill out applications. That will save a lot of time and avoid many complications. If you are still confused and have questions for which you can't find answers, see a college financial aid administrator or community counselor.

Be diligent. Have a written list of questions to ask when speaking to a counselor or financial aid administrator. When you talk to someone, ask for and write down his or her name and title. Persist in your questions until you understand. Keep a record of everything you do. Work for your rightful benefits.

COMPARISON GUIDE

Institutions vary in the amount and type of aid they offer to adults. This Comparison Guide gives you an idea of the right questions to ask when you are comparing financial aid at different institutions. After you've filled out the Comparison Guide, compare your total cost at the institution you are most interested in attending. Are you willing to pay more for one college than another? Considering any other financial aid income that may be available to you, will you be able to afford the college that interests you the most?

If the college indicates that you have some financial need it cannot meet in its financial aid offer, you will have to cover this amount yourself either by cutting your costs, if possible, or through special aid programs or with an educational loan or other form of borrowing.

Whether you will need a lot of aid or just a little, colleges will attempt to help you find the combination of resources you need to attend. Talk it over with a financial aid administrator or counselor.

Comparison Guide

	INSTITUTION 1	INSTITUTION 2	INSTITUTION 3	INSTITUTION 4
Name of the institution you are considering	_____	_____	_____	_____
Name of the financial aid administrator	_____	_____	_____	_____
Office hours	_____	_____	_____	_____
Telephone number	_____	_____	_____	_____

Aid Programs

	INSTITUTION 1	INSTITUTION 2	INSTITUTION 3	INSTITUTION 4
Is the institution eligible to award federal and state student aid?	_____	_____	_____	_____
Does it participate in all the federal and state programs?	_____	_____	_____	_____

Does it offer any aid programs of its own?

Would I qualify?

Does it offer any loans?

Policies and Practices

What formal or informal practices are used to award aid?

What types of students receive first preference?

Does the institution have a deferred tuition policy?

Does it offer advanced standing?

Can I use my credit card for tuition, fees, and in book stores?

Is there convenient public transportation to campus?

	INSTITUTION 1	INSTITUTION 2	INSTITUTION 3	INSTITUTION 4
Will I need a car to get back and forth to college?	_____	_____	_____	_____
When must I pay tuition fees?	_____	_____	_____	_____
Application fees?	_____	_____	_____	_____
Academic fees?	_____	_____	_____	_____
Laboratory fees?	_____	_____	_____	_____
Room rent?	_____	_____	_____	_____
Other?	_____	_____	_____	_____
Other?	_____	_____	_____	_____
Is there an installment tuition plan?	_____	_____	_____	_____
Do I qualify for any type of waiver?	_____	_____	_____	_____
Are tuition reductions made available?	_____	_____	_____	_____
Can I get a package price, two courses for the price of one, or a similar arrangement?	_____	_____	_____	_____

Forms and Deadlines

What is the admissions deadline, if any? (see "Application Checklist," page 18)

What is the financial aid deadline, if any?

Is there a preferred deadline?

What financial aid forms are required?

What form should I use for a Pell Grant?

Where should I send the completed application?

Are there other forms I must use?

Costs	INSTITUTION 1	INSTITUTION 2	INSTITUTION 3	INSTITUTION 4
1. Tuition and fees	_____	_____	_____	_____
2. Books and supplies	_____	_____	_____	_____
3. Student's housing	_____	_____	_____	_____
4. Student's meals*	_____	_____	_____	_____
5. Personal (clothing, laundry, recreation, medical)	_____	_____	_____	_____
6. Transportation**	_____	_____	_____	_____
7. Other (such as costs of child care, extra expenses because of handicap)	_____	_____	_____	_____
8. Total budget (add 1 through 7)	_____	_____	_____	_____

Aid Awards

	INSTITUTION 1	INSTITUTION 2	INSTITUTION 3	INSTITUTION 4
Total expense budget	_____	_____	_____	_____
Minus expected student and spouse contribution	_____	_____	_____	_____

Equals net need to attend the
institution   _____   _____

Minus grant aid offered by the
institution   _____   _____

Minus loan offered   _____   _____

Minus work-study offered   _____   _____

Equals unmet need   _____   _____

* You will want to consider these expenses to your family if you live at home.
** If you are planning to live on campus, you should estimate the cost of the round trips you will make
to your home. Colleges usually estimate that a student makes two or three round trips during the
year. Students living at home should figure the costs of daily transportation to the college.

Financial Aid Calendar

January

This is the best time to begin investigating: Find a counselor, ask questions, look at educational options and special-purpose programs. If you start now, you'll have plenty of time.

February

May

June

September

October

Be sure to write for admissions and financial aid materials from schools you are interested in.

Year One

March	April
	Save a copy of your tax return for possible later assistance in filling out financial aid forms.

July	August

November	December

Financial Aid Calendar

January

Get your application for a Pell Grant, and apply any time after January 1. Even if you are using the same form to apply for other aid, don't file the form until after January 1.

February

Pick up any other applications and forms you will need. Remember to mark this calendar and meet each deadline for each program for which you apply.

May

Respond to admissions office about your plans to enroll or not to enroll.

June

Complete GSL application if needed. Return accepted/declined/revised offer of aid.

September

Begin your academic program.

October

Year Two

March

April

Offers of financial aid are generally sent in April–May if you applied in January. Respond with a copy of your tax return if requested.

July

August

November

Find out deadline dates for filing for aid for the next school year and when you may pick up forms.

December

10

Sources
of
Financial
Aid
Information

LOCATING COUNSELING SERVICES

For assistance in locating counseling services, contact the following agencies:

Catalyst
14 East 60 Street
New York, New York 10022

National Center for Educational Brokering
325 Ninth Street
San Francisco, California 94103

RESOURCES ON ADULT LEARNING

Back to School: A College Guide for Adults, by William C. Haponski and Charles E. McCabe, 1982. Peterson's Guides, P.O. Box 2123, Princeton, New Jersey 08540. Offers comprehensive guidance, from overcoming initial fears about college to graduation. Gives profiles of successful adult students, along with several appendices on financial aid and sources for further information, bibliographies of guides to colleges and career information, and a glossary of terms.

A Consumer's Guide to Colleges for the Adult Learner, by Sharon Hayenga, Laura Adams, and Norma Rowe. CAEL Publications, Lakefront North, Suite 300, Columbia, Maryland 21044.

Happier by Degrees: A College Reentry Guide for Women, by Pam Mendelsohn, E. P. Dutton, 2 Park Avenue, New York, New York 10016. An extensive sourcebook for women who are considering going back to school.

Learning Times, a newspaper for adult learners published by the Office of Adult Learning Services, The College

Board. Ask for a free copy at the local library or nearby college financial aid office.

Lifelong Learner, The, by Ronald Gross. Simon and Schuster, Inc., 1230 Avenue of the Americas, New York, New York 10020. An introduction to adult learning resources. Ask for a copy at the local library.

New Paths to Learning: College Education for Adults, by Ronald Gross. Public Affairs Pamphlet No. 546, available from the Public Affairs Committee, 381 Park Avenue South, New York, New York 10016. A brief account of nontraditional ways to continue your education, including independent study, learning via television, and weekend college.

Senior Learning Times, a newspaper for senior citizens published by the Office of Adult Learning Services, The College Board. Ask for a copy at the local library.

So You Want to Go Back to School: Facing the Realities of Reentry, by Elinor Lenz and Marjorie Hansen Shaevitz, McGraw-Hill Book Company, Book Distribution Center, Hightstown, New Jersey 08520. This book is a classic text on coping with the problems of reentry to higher education.

CREDIT-BY-EXAMINATION PROGRAMS

Advanced Placement Examinations
The College Board
888 Seventh Avenue
New York, New York 10106

College-Level Examination Program (CLEP) of the College Board. Ask the admissions counselor or testing center director at any college or university for further information on CLEP.

New York College Proficiency Examination Program
New York State Education Department
Cultural Education Center
Albany, New York 12230

Regents External Degree Program
The University of the State of New York
Cultural Education Center
Albany, New York 12230

For information on New York State College Proficiency Examinations and Regents External Degree Examinations administered outside New York State, write to:

ACT PEP
P.O. Box 168
Iowa City, Iowa 52243

Guide to Credit by Examination. American Council on Education, Publication Sales, Section 0061, Suite 30, One Dupont Circle, N.W., Washington, D.C. 20036.

CREDIT FOR PRIOR LEARNING

Assessing Prior Learning — A CAEL Student Guide, by Aubrey Forrest. CAEL Publications, Lakefront North, Suite 300, Columbia, Maryland 21044.

Guide to the Evaluation of Educational Experiences in the Armed Services, 1980 edition, published biennially. American Council on Education, Publication Sales, Section 0061, Suite 30, One Dupont Circle, N.W., Washington, D.C. 20036.

National Guide to Educational Credit for Training Programs, The, 1980 edition, published annually. American Council on Education, Publication Sales, Section 0061, Suite 30, One Dupont Circle, N.W., Washington, D.C. 20036.

Student Guide to Portfolio Development. CAEL Publications, Lakefront North, Suite 300, Columbia, Maryland 21044.

Wherever You Learned It: A Directory of Opportunities for Educational Credit (5 volumes), by Valerie McIntyre and edited by Ruth Cargo. CAEL Publications, Lakefront North, Suite 300, Columbia, Maryland 21044.

You Deserve the Credit: A Student Guide to Receiving Credit for Noncollege Learning. CAEL Publications, Lakefront North, Suite 300, Columbia, Maryland 21044.

EXTERNAL DEGREE PROGRAMS

Board of State Academic Awards
340 Capitol Avenue
Hartford, Connecticut 06115

The Board of Governors
Bachelor of Arts Degree Program
544 Illes Park Place
Springfield, Illinois 62706

Thomas A. Edison College
Kelsey Building
101 West State Street
Trenton, New Jersey 08625

Regents External Degree Program
The University of the State of New York
Cultural Education Center
Albany, New York 12230

Guide to Undergraduate External Degree Programs in the United States. American Council on Education, Publication Sales, Section 0061, Suite 30, One Dupont Circle, N.W., Washington, D.C. 20036.

NONTRADITIONAL DEGREE PROGRAMS AND CORRESPONDENCE STUDY

Alternative Guide to College Degrees and Nontraditional Higher Education, by John Bjorn Bear. The Stonesong Press, a division of Grosset & Dunlap, 51 Madison Avenue, New York, New York 10010.

Bear's Guide to Non-Traditional College Degrees, seventh edition, by John Bear, Ph.D. Bear's Guides, P.O. Box 646, Mendocino, California 95460.

Directory of Accredited Home Study Schools. National Home Study Council, 1601 18th Street, N.W., Washington, D.C. 20009. Free. The National Home Study Council also offers the following free publications on the subject of college degrees through home study: *The ABC's of Earning College Credit through Home Study; List of Agencies with Information on College Credit without Going to College; A Counselor's Guide to Home Study.*

Guide to Independent Study through Correspondence Instruction 1980–82, edited by Joan H. Hunter. Peterson's Guides, Department 6291, P.O. Box 978, Edison, New Jersey 08817.

Tips on Home Study Schools. This is available free of charge by sending a stamped, self-addressed, number 10 envelope to the Council of Better Business Bureaus, Inc., 1150 17th Street, N.W., Washington, D.C. 20036.

TUITION BENEFIT PROGRAMS

These publications offer assistance in locating employee and union tuition benefit programs and programs for financing part-time students.

College Financial Aid and the Employee Tuition Benefit Programs of the Fortune 500 Companies, by Joseph O'Neill. Conference University Press, Box 24, Princeton, New Jersey 08540. Information about employee educational benefits from 358 companies, and comprehensive data about financial aid programs available to part-time students at 430 colleges listed alphabetically by state.

The AFL-CIO Guide to Union Sponsored Scholarships and Awards, 1982 edition. Available free from Department of Education, AFL-CIO, 815 16th Street, N.W., Washington, D.C. 20006.

FEDERAL STUDENT FINANCIAL AID PROGRAMS

For general information about federal and state student aid programs, your eligibility for aid, financial aid counseling, and help in completing your applications for federal student aid programs, communicate with the Federal Student Aid Programs, P.O. Box 84, Washington, D.C. 20044.

The Student Guide: Five Federal Financial Aid Programs, published annually. A free copy of the latest edition is available from Federal Student Aid Programs, P.O. Box 84, Washington, D.C. 20044.

Federal Financial Aid for Men and Women Resuming Their Education. or Training. A guide for nontraditional students, available free from Federal Student Aid Programs, P.O. Box 84, Washington, D.C. 20044.

OPTIONS PROGRAM

The Student Loan Marketing Association (Sallie Mae) offers an OPTIONS program that enables borrowers who owe more than $5,000 in student loans under three federal programs—the Guaranteed Student Loan Program (GSL), Federally Insured Student Loan Program (FISL), and National Direct Student Loan Program (NDSL)—to consolidate and/or refinance their indebtedness into a single new loan at seven percent interest from Sallie Mae. The new loan is insured by the U.S. Department of Education and usually has a longer repayment term (up to 20 years) than the original loans. Three repayment plans are offered, including two different graduated payment plans and a fixed payment plan. OPTIONS assists borrowers by helping them reduce their monthly student loan payments. Participants thus far have been able to reduce the amount of their monthly loan payments for the first few years of the agreement by 40 percent. For further information on OPTIONS, write to the Student Loan Marketing Association, Loan Consolidation Program, Suite 175, 1050 Thomas Jefferson Street, N.W., Washington, D.C. 20007.

EDUCATIONAL OPPORTUNITY CENTERS AND THE SPECIAL SERVICES PROGRAM

Educational Opportunity Centers and the Talent Search Program are funded by the federal Higher Education Act to provide specific services to low-income youth or adults who will be first generation college students. Educational Opportunity Centers serve adults who qualify as low-income or first generation college students who may need information on financial aid, academic assistance, application for admission to postsecondary educational institutions, counseling, tutorial, and other necessary assistance. You must be a citizen or national of the United States and meet the requirements for eligibility.

The Special Services for Disadvantaged Students Program (SS) is designed to assist enrolled students who are eligible by means of income and their first generation college status to complete their postsecondary education program. An SS project may provide tutoring, counseling, remedial instruction, and other educational and special services. Projects are located throughout the country on college campuses. For further information, check with the admissions office of the college you are considering. For information on the nearest Educational Opportunity Center or Special Services for Disadvantaged Students Program, call the Office of Institutional Support Programs, Division of Student Services, U.S. Department of Education, at 202–245–2511, weekdays between 8 a.m. and 4 p.m., Eastern time, or write to the Information Systems and Program Support Branch, OISP/DSS, Room 3514, ROB-3, U.S. Department of Education, 400 Maryland Avenue, S.W., Washington, D.C. 20202.

GENERAL SOURCES

Don't Miss Out: The Ambitious Student's Guide to Scholarships and Loans, sixth edition, 1981–83, by Robert Leider. Octameron Association, Inc., P.O. Box 3437, Alexandria, Virginia 22302.

Financial Aid for College Students: Sources of Information, 1981. American Chemical Society, Education Department, 1155 16th Street, N.W., Washington, D.C. 20036. Updated biennially, first copy free. This contains a selected bibliography and a list of grant programs.

Need a Lift?, 1982. The American Legion, P.O. Box 1055, Attention: Emblem Sales Division, Indianapolis, Indiana 46206. Updated annually. Listed are sources of career, scholarship, and loan information for all students, with emphasis on scholarship opportunities for veterans, dependents of veterans, and children of deceased or disabled veterans.

SPECIFIC POPULATION GROUPS

Career Development Opportunities for Native Americans, 1975. Bureau of Indian Affairs, Division of Postsecondary Education, 1951 Constitution Avenue, Washington, D.C. 20245. This free publication lists approximately 100 sources of assistance for students who are at least one-fourth Indian, Eskimo, or Aleut of a tribal group recognized by the Bureau of Indian Affairs for certain benefits. This booklet is currently being updated.

Directory of Financial Aids for Women, 1978. Gail Ann Schlachter, Reference Service Press, 9023 Alcott Street, Suite 201, Los Angeles, California 90035. This is a listing of scholarships, fellowships, loans, grants, internships, awards, and prizes designed primarily or exclusively for women. Also included are listings of women's credit unions and state sources of educational benefits.

Directory of Special Programs for Minority Group Members: Career Information Services, Employment Skills Banks, Financial Aid Sources, 1980, third edition, Willis Johnson, ed.

Garrett Park Press, Garrett Park, Maryland 20896. This is a companion to the Garrett Park Press publications that follow.

The following books, listing financial aid sources for minority students in specific fields of study, were edited by Michele Wilson and published by Garrett Park Press, Garrett Park, Maryland, 1980–81.

Financial Aid for Minorities in Allied Health
Financial Aid for Minorities in Business
Financial Aid for Minorities in Education
Financial Aid for Minorities in Journalism/Communications
Financial Aid for Minorities in Law
Financial Aid for Minorities in Science
Financial Aid for Minorities in Medicine
Financial Aid for Minorities in Engineering

Graduate School Information Aids, 1981. American Chemical Society, Education Department, 1155 16th Street, N.W., Washington, D.C. 20036. First copy free. This contains a selected bibliography and a list of grant programs.

Grants Register, 1981–83, 1980. St. Martin's Press, 175 Fifth Avenue, New York, New York 10010. Updated biennially, this publication lists scholarships and fellowships at all levels of graduate study. Specific awards are included for refugees, war veterans, minorities, and students in unexpected financial difficulties.

Selected List of Postsecondary Education Opportunities for Minorities and Women, 1981. U.S. Government Printing Office, Washington, D.C. 20402 (#065–000–00118–7). Updated annually, this publication lists education opportunities for minorities and women at the postsecondary level by fields of study. It also provides general information about seeking assistance in pursuing additional education and career goals.

SOURCES OF INFORMATION ON GUARANTEED STUDENT LOANS AND STATE STUDENT AID

ALABAMA
ALABAMA COMMISSION
ON HIGHER EDUCATION
1 Court Square, Suite 221
Montgomery, Alabama 36197
GSL and State Aid:
(205) 832–3790

ALASKA
ALASKA COMMISSION
ON POSTSECONDARY
EDUCATION
400 Willoughby Avenue
Pouch F P
Juneau, Alaska 99801
GSL and State Aid:
(907) 465–2962

ARIZONA
GSL: Arizona Educational Loan
Program
801 East Virginia Avenue
Phoenix, Arizona 85004
(602) 252–5793

State Aid: ARIZONA
COMMISSION FOR POST-
SECONDARY EDUCATION
1937 West Jefferson
Phoenix, Arizona 85009
(602) 255–3109

ARKANSAS
GSL: STUDENT LOAN
GUARANTEE FOUNDA-
TIONS OF ARKANSAS
1515 West Seventh Street,
Suite 515
Little Rock, Arkansas 72202
(501) 371–2634

State Aid: DEPARTMENT OF
HIGHER EDUCATION
1301 West Seventh Street
Little Rock, Arkansas 72201
(501) 371–1441, Ext. 56

CALIFORNIA
CALIFORNIA STUDENT
AID COMMISSION
1410 Fifth Street
Sacramento, California 95814
GSL: (916) 322–0435
State Aid: (916) 445–0880

COLORADO
GSL: COLORADO
GUARANTEED STUDENT
LOAN PROGRAM
7000 North Broadway, Suite 100
Denver, Colorado 80221
(303) 427–0259

State Aid: COLORADO
COMMISSION ON HIGHER
EDUCATION
1550 Lincoln Street, Room 210
Denver, Colorado 80203
(303) 866–2748

CONNECTICUT
GSL: CONNECTICUT
STUDENT LOAN
FOUNDATION
25 Pratt Street
Hartford, Connecticut 06103
(203) 547–1510

State Aid: CONNECTICUT
BOARD OF HIGHER
EDUCATION
61 Woodland Street
Hartford, Connecticut 06105
(203) 566-6218

DELAWARE
GSL: DELAWARE HIGHER
EDUCATION LOAN
PROGRAM
c/o Brandywine College
Box 7139
Wilmington, Delaware 19803
(302) 478-3000, Ext. 201

State Aid: DELAWARE
POSTSECONDARY EDU-
CATION COMMISSION
Carvel State Office Building
220 French Street
Wilmington, Delaware 19801
(302) 571-3240

DISTRICT OF COLUMBIA
GSL: HIGHER EDUCA-
TION ASSISTANCE
FOUNDATION
HIGHER EDUCATION
LOAN PROGRAM (HELP)
OF D.C., INC.
1001 Connecticut Avenue,
N.W.
Suite 825
Washington, D.C. 20036
(202) 861-0701

State Aid: OFFICE OF
STATE EDUCATION
AFFAIRS
614 H Street, N.W.
8th Floor, Room 817
Washington, D.C. 20001
(202) 727-3688

FLORIDA
FLORIDA STUDENT
FINANCIAL ASSISTANCE
COMMISSION
Knott Building
Tallahassee, Florida 32301
GSL and State Aid:
(904) 487-1800

GEORGIA
GEORGIA HIGHER
EDUCATION ASSISTANCE
CORPORATION
9 LaVista Perimeter Park
2187 Northlake Parkway
Suite 110
Tucker, Georgia 30084
GSL: (404) 393-7241
State Aid: (404) 393-7253

HAWAII
GSL: HAWAII EDUCATION
LOAN PROGRAM
1314 South King Street,
Suite 603
Honolulu, Hawaii 96814
(808) 536-3731

State Aid: STATE POST-
SECONDARY EDUCATION
COMMISSION
124F Bachman Hall
University of Hawaii
2444 Dole Street
Honolulu, Hawaii 96822
(808) 948-6862

IDAHO
GSL: STUDENT LOAN
FUND OF IDAHO, INC.
Processing Center
Route 2, North Whitley Drive
Fruitland, Idaho 83619
(208) 452–4058

State Aid: OFFICE OF
STATE BOARD OF
EDUCATION
650 West State Street, Room 307
Boise, Idaho 83720
(208) 334–2270

ILLINOIS
GSL: ILLINOIS GUARAN-
TEED LOAN PROGRAM
102 Wilmot Road
Deerfield, Illinois 60015
(312) 945–7040

State Aid: ILLINOIS STATE
SCHOLARSHIP COM-
MISSION
102 Wilmot Road
Deerfield, Illinois 60015
(312) 948–8550

INDIANA
STATE STUDENT
ASSISTANCE COMMIS-
SION OF INDIANA
219 North Senate Avenue,
1st Floor
Indianapolis, Indiana 46202
GSL: (317) 232–2366
State Aid: (317) 232–2351

IOWA
IOWA COLLEGE AID
COMMISSION
201 Jewett Building
Ninth and Grand
Des Moines, Iowa 50309
GSL: (515) 281–8537
State Aid: (515) 281–3501

KANSAS
GSL: HIGHER EDUCATION
ASSISTANCE
FOUNDATION
34 Corporate Woods
10950 Grand View Drive
Overland Park, Kansas 66210
(913) 648–4255

State Aid: BOARD OF
REGENTS – STATE OF
KANSAS
1416 Merchants National Bank
Topeka, Kansas 66612
(913) 296–3421

KENTUCKY
KENTUCKY HIGHER
EDUCATION ASSISTANCE
AUTHORITY
1050 U.S. 127 South
West Frankfort Office Complex
Frankfort, Kentucky 40601
GSL and State Aid:
(502) 564–7990

LOUISIANA
GOVERNOR'S SPECIAL
COMMISSION ON
EDUCATION SERVICES
4637 Jamestown Street
Box 44127
Baton Rouge, Louisiana 70804
GSL and State Aid:
(504) 925–3630

MAINE

STATE DEPARTMENT OF
EDUCATIONAL AND
CULTURAL SERVICES
Division of Higher Education
Services
State House Station 23
Augusta, Maine 04333
GSL and State Aid:
(207) 289-2183

MARYLAND

GSL: MARYLAND HIGHER
EDUCATION LOAN
CORPORATION
2100 Guilford Avenue
Baltimore, Maryland 21218
(301) 659-6555

State Aid: MARYLAND
STATE SCHOLARSHIP
BOARD
2100 Guilford Avenue
Baltimore, Maryland 21218
(301) 659-6420

MASSACHUSETTS

GSL: MASSACHUSETTS
HIGHER EDUCATION
ASSISTANCE COR-
PORATION
330 Stuart Street
Boston, Massachusetts 02116
(617) 426-9796

State Aid: MASSACHUSETTS
BOARD OF REGENTS OF
HIGHER EDUCATION
Scholarship Office
330 Stuart Street
Boston, Massachusetts 02116
(617) 727-9420

MICHIGAN

GSL: MICHIGAN DEPART-
MENT OF EDUCATION
Guaranteed Student Loan
Program
Box 30047
Lansing, Michigan 48909
(517) 373-0760

State Aid: MICHIGAN
DEPARTMENT OF
EDUCATION
Box 30008
Lansing, Michigan 48909
(517) 373-3394

MINNESOTA

GSL: HIGHER EDUCATION
ASSISTANCE FOUN-
DATION
900 American National Bank
Building
Fifth and Minnesota Streets
St. Paul, Minnesota 55101
(612) 227-7661

State Aid: MINNESOTA
HIGHER EDUCATION
COORDINATING BOARD
400 Capitol Square
550 Cedar Street
St. Paul, Minnesota 55101
(612) 296-3974

MISSISSIPPI

GSL: BOARD OF TRUSTEES
OF STATE INSTITUTIONS
OF HIGHER LEARNING
3825 Ridgewood Road
Box 2336
Jackson, Mississippi 39205
(601) 982-6611

State Aid: MISSISSIPPI
POSTSECONDARY EDU-
CATION FINANCIAL
ASSISTANCE BOARD
Box 2336
Jackson, Mississippi 39205
(601) 982–6168

MISSOURI
GSL: MISSOURI DEPART-
MENT OF HIGHER
EDUCATION
Box 1438
Jefferson City, Missouri 65102
(314) 751–3940

State Aid: MISSOURI
DEPARTMENT OF
HIGHER EDUCATION
Box 1437
Jefferson City, Missouri 65102
(314) 751–3940

MONTANA
GSL and State Aid:
MONTANA UNIVERSITY
SYSTEM
33 South Last Chance Gulch
Helena, Montana 59601
(406) 449–3024

NEBRASKA
Cornhusker Bank Building
Eleventh and Cornhusker
Highway
Suite 304
Lincoln, Nebraska 68521
(402) 476–9129

State Aid: NEBRASKA
COORDINATING COMMIS-
SION FOR POSTSECOND-
ARY EDUCATION
301 Centennial Mall South
Box 95005
Lincoln, Nebraska 68509
(402) 471–2847

NEVADA
GSL: NEVADA STATE
DEPARTMENT OF EDUCA-
TION
400 West King Street
Carson City, Nevada 89710
(702) 885–3107

State Aid: UNIVERSITY OF
NEVADA SYSTEM
405 Marsh Avenue
Reno, Nevada 89509
(702) 784–4666

NEW HAMPSHIRE
GSL: NEW HAMPSHIRE
HIGHER EDUCATION
ASSISTANCE FOUNDA-
TION
143 North Main Street
Box 877
Concord, New Hampshire 03301
(603) 225–6612

State Aid: NEW HAMPSHIRE
POSTSECONDARY EDU-
CATION COMMISSION
61 South Spring Street
Concord, New Hampshire 03301
(603) 271-2555

NEW JERSEY
GSL: NEW JERSEY
HIGHER EDUCATION
ASSISTANCE AUTHORITY
C. N. 00538
Trenton, New Jersey 08638
(609) 292–3906

State Aid: DEPARTMENT OF HIGHER EDUCATION
Office of Student Assistance
Number 4 Quakerbridge Plaza
C. N. 540
Trenton, New Jersey 08625
(609) 292-4646

NEW MEXICO
GSL: NEW MEXICO EDU-CATIONAL ASSISTANCE FOUNDATION
2301 Yale, S.E., Building F
Albuquerque, New Mexico 87106
(505) 277-6304

State Aid: BOARD OF EDUCATION FINANCE
1068 Cerrillos Road
Santa Fe, New Mexico 87503
(505) 827-5017

NEW YORK
NEW YORK STATE HIGHER EDUCATION SERVICES CORPORATION
99 Washington Avenue
Albany, New York 12255
GSL: (518) 473-1574
State Aid: (518) 474-5642

NORTH CAROLINA
NORTH CAROLINA STATE EDUCATION ASSISTANCE AUTHORITY
Box 2688
Chapel Hill, North Carolina 27514
GSL and State Aid:
(919) 473-1688

NORTH DAKOTA
GSL: STUDENT FINAN-CIAL ASSISTANCE DEPARTMENT OF EDUCATION
11037 Federal Office Building
Nineteenth and Stout Streets
Denver, Colorado 80294
(303) 837-3676

State Aid: NORTH DAKOTA STUDENT FINANCIAL ASSISTANCE PROGRAM
10th Floor, State Capitol
Bismarck, North Dakota 58505
(701) 224-4114

OHIO
GSL: OHIO STUDENT LOAN COMMISSION
Box 16610
Columbus, Ohio 43216
(614) 466-3091

State Aid: OHIO BOARD OF REGENTS
3600 State Office Tower
30 East Broad Street
Columbus, Ohio 43215
(614) 466-7420

OKLAHOMA
OKLAHOMA STATE REGENTS FOR HIGHER EDUCATION
500 Education Building
State Capitol Complex
Oklahoma City,
Oklahoma 73105
GSL and State Aid:
(405) 521-8262

OREGON
OREGON STATE
SCHOLARSHIP COMMIS-
SION
1445 Willamette Street
Eugene, Oregon 97401
GSL: (800) 452–8807 (within
OR), (503) 686–3200
State Aid: (503) 686–4166

PENNSYLVANIA
PENNSYLVANIA HIGHER
EDUCATION ASSISTANCE
AGENCY
660 Boas Street
Harrisburg, Pennsylvania 17102
GSL: (800) 692–7392 (within
PA), (717) 787–1932
State Aid: (800) 692–7435
(within PA), (717) 787–1937

RHODE ISLAND
RHODE ISLAND HIGHER
EDUCATION ASSISTANCE
AUTHORITY
274 Weybosset Street
Providence, Rhode Island 02903
GSL and State Aid:
(401) 277–2050

SOUTH CAROLINA
GSL: SOUTH CAROLINA
STUDENT LOAN
CORPORATION
Interstate Center, Suite 210
Box 21337
Columbia, South Carolina 29221
(803) 798–0916

State Aid: HIGHER
EDUCATION TUITION
GRANTS AGENCY
411 Keenan Building
Box 11638
Columbia, South Carolina 29211
(803) 758–7070

SOUTH DAKOTA
GSL: SOUTH DAKOTA
EDUCATION ASSISTANCE
CORPORATION
105 First Ave., S.W.
Aberdeen, South Dakota 57401
(605) 225–6423

State Aid: DEPARTMENT
OF EDUCATION AND
CULTURAL AFFAIRS
Richard F. Kneip Building
Pierre, South Dakota 57501
(605) 773–3134

TENNESSEE
TENNESSEE STUDENT
ASSISTANCE CORPORA-
TION
B-3 Capitol Towers, Suite 9
Nashville, Tennessee 37219
GSL and State Aid:
(800) 342–1663 (within Tenn.),
(615) 741–1346

TEXAS
GSL: TEXAS GUARAN-
TEED STUDENT LOAN
CORPORATION
Champion Tower, Suite 510
Austin, Texas 78752
(512) 835–1900

State Aid: COORDINATING
BOARD TEXAS COLLEGE
AND UNIVERSITY
SYSTEM
Box 12788, Capitol Station
Austin, Texas 78711
(512) 475–8169

UTAH
GSL: UTAH EDUCATION
LOAN SERVICE
1800 South West Temple
Suite 101
Salt Lake City, Utah 84108
(801) 486-5921

State Aid: UTAH STATE
BOARD OF REGENTS
807 East South Temple
Suite 204
Salt Lake City, Utah 84102
(801) 533-5617

VERMONT
VERMONT STUDENT
ASSISTANCE CORPORA-
TION
5 Burlington Square
Burlington, Vermont 05401
GSL and State Aid:
(800) 642-3177 (within VT),
(802) 658-4530

VIRGINIA
GSL: VIRGINIA STATE
EDUCATION ASSISTANCE
AUTHORITY
6 North Sixth Street
Suite 400
Richmond, Virginia 23219
(804) 786-2035

State Aid: STATE COUNCIL
OF HIGHER EDUCATION
FOR VIRGINIA
James Monroe Building
101 North 14th Street
Richmond, Virginia 23219
(804) 225-2141

WASHINGTON
GSL: WASHINGTON
STUDENT LOAN
GUARANTY ASSOCIA-
TION
100 South King Street, Suite 560
Westland Building
Seattle, Washington 98104
(206) 625-1030

State Aid: COUNCIL FOR
POSTSECONDARY EDU-
CATION
908 East Fifth Avenue
Olympia, Washington 98504
(206) 753-3571

WEST VIRGINIA
GSL: HIGHER EDUCA-
TION ASSISTANCE
FOUNDATION
HIGHER EDUCATION
LOAN PROGRAM OF
WEST VIRGINIA, INC.
P.O. Box 591
Union Building, Suite 900
723 Kanawha Boulevard East
Charleston, West Virginia 25322
(304) 345-7211

State Aid: WEST VIRGINIA
BOARD OF REGENTS
950 Kanawha Boulevard East
Charleston, West Virginia 25301
(304) 348-0112

WISCONSIN
GSL: WISCONSIN HIGHER
EDUCATION CORPORA-
TION
137 East Wilson Street
Madison, Wisconsin 53702
(608) 266-1653

State Aid: WISCONSIN
HIGHER EDUCATIONAL
AIDS BOARD
Box 7858
Madison, Wisconsin 53707
(608) 266–2897

WYOMING

GSL: HIGHER EDUCATION
ASSISTANCE FOUNDA-
TION
American National Bank
Building
20 Street at Capitol, Suite 320
Cheyenne, Wyoming 82001
(307) 635–3259

State Aid: WYOMING
COMMUNITY COLLEGE
COMMISSION
1720 Carey Avenue
Boyd Building, Fifth Floor
Cheyenne, Wyoming 82002
(307) 777–7763

AMERICAN SAMOA

GSL: STUDENT FINAN-
CIAL ASSISTANCE
U.S. DEPARTMENT OF
EDUCATION
50 United Nations Plaza,
Rm. 250, San Francisco,
California (415) 556–0137

State Aid: DEPARTMENT
OF EDUCATION
GOVERNMENT OF
AMERICAN SAMOA
Pago Pago, American Samoa
96799
(Overseas) 633–4256

COMMONWEALTH OF THE NORTHERN MARIANA ISLANDS

GSL: See American Samoa

State Aid: DEPARTMENT
OF EDUCATION
COMMONWEALTH OF
THE NORTHERN
MARIANA ISLANDS
Saipan, Mariana Islands 96950
(Saipan) 9812/9311

GUAM

GSL: See American Samoa

State Aid: UNIVERSITY OF
GUAM
Box EK
Agana, Guam 96910
(734) 2177

PUERTO RICO

GSL: STUDENT FINAN-
CIAL ASSISTANCE
DEPARTMENT OF
EDUCATION
26 Federal Plaza
New York, New York 10007
(212) 264–4022

State Aid: COUNCIL ON
HIGHER EDUCATION
Box F-UPR Station
Rio Piedras, Puerto Rico 00931
(809) 751–5082/1136

TRUST TERRITORY OF THE PACIFIC ISLANDS AND WAKE ISLAND

GSL: See American Samoa

State Aid: OFFICE OF THE HIGH COMMISSIONER, TRUST TERRITORY OF THE PACIFIC ISLANDS
Saipan, Mariana Islands 96950
(Saipan) 9870

VIRGIN ISLANDS

BOARD OF EDUCATION
Box 9128
St. Thomas, Virgin Islands 00801
GSL and State Aid:
(809) 774-4546

USAF, INC.

(800) 227-3037 (West Coast)
(800) 382-4506 (Indiana only)
(800) 428-9250 (All other states)
UNITED STUDENT AID FUNDS PROCESSING CENTER
Box 50827
Indianapolis, Indiana 46250

STATE HIGHER EDUCATION EXECUTIVE AGENCIES

ALABAMA
Commission on Higher
Education
One Court Square, #221
Montgomery, Alabama 36104
(205) 832-6555

ALASKA
Alaska Commission on
Postsecondary Education
Pouch F – State Office Building
Juneau, Alaska 99811
(907) 465-2854

ARIZONA
State Board of Regents
1535 West Jefferson
Phoenix, Arizona 85007
(602) 255-4082

ARKANSAS
Department of Higher
Education
1301 West Seventh Street
Little Rock, Arkansas 72201
(501) 371-1441

CALIFORNIA
California Postsecondary
Education Commission
1020 Twelfth Street
Sacramento, California 95814
(916) 445-7933

COLORADO
Commission on Higher
Education
1550 Lincoln Street, #210
Denver, Colorado 80203
(303) 866-4034

CONNECTICUT
Board of Higher Education
61 Woodland Street
Hartford, Connecticut 06105
(203) 566-5766

DELAWARE
Delaware Postsecondary
Education Commission
Carvel State Office Building
820 French Street
Wilmington, Delaware 19801
(302) 571-3240

DISTRICT OF COLUMBIA
Commission on Postsecondary
Education
614 H Street, N.W., #817
Washington, D.C. 20001
(202) 727-3685

FLORIDA
State Department of Education
Knott Building
Tallahassee, Florida 32301
(904) 488-0816

GEORGIA
Regents of the University
System
244 Washington Street, S.W.
Atlanta, Georgia 30334
(404) 656–2200

HAWAII
University of Hawaii
2444 Dole Street
Honolulu, Hawaii 96822
(808) 948–8207

IDAHO
State Board of Education
Len B. Jordan Building, Suite 307
650 West State Street
Boise, Idaho 83720
(208) 334–2270

ILLINOIS
Board of Higher Education
500 Reisch Building
4 West Old Capitol Square
Springfield, Illinois 62701
(217) 782–2551

INDIANA
Commission for Higher
Education
143 West Market Street
Indianapolis, Indiana 46202
(317) 232–1900

IOWA
Board of Regents
Lucas State Office Building
Des Moines, Iowa 50319
(515) 281–3934

KANSAS
Board of Regents
Merchants National Bank Tower
800 Jackson, #1416
Topeka, Kansas 66612
(913) 296–3421

KENTUCKY
Council on Higher Education
West Frankfort Office Complex
U.S. 127 South
Frankfort, Kentucky 40601
(502) 564–3553

LOUISIANA
State Board of Regents
161 Riverside Mall
Baton Rouge, Louisiana 70801
(504) 342–4253

MAINE
University of Maine
107 Maine Avenue
Bangor, Maine 04401
(207) 947–0336

MARYLAND
State Board for Higher
Education
16 Francis Street
Annapolis, Maryland 21401
(301) 269–2971

MASSACHUSETTS
Massachusetts Board of Regents
1 Ashburton Place, #619
Boston, Massachusetts 02108
(617) 727–7785

MINNESOTA
Higher Education Coordinating
Board
550 Cedar Street, Suite 400
St. Paul, Minnesota 55101
(612) 296–9665

MISSISSIPPI
Board of Trustees of State
Institutions of Higher Learning
Box 2336
Jackson, Mississippi 39205
(601) 982–6611

MISSOURI
Department of Higher Education
600 Monroe Street
Jefferson City, Missouri 65101
(314) 751–2361

MONTANA
Board of Regents of Higher
Education
33 South Last Chance Gulch
Helena, Montana 59601
(406) 449–3024

NEBRASKA
Nebraska Coordinating
Commission
for Postsecondary Education
301 Centennial Mall South
Box 95005
Lincoln, Nebraska 68509
(402) 471–2847

NEVADA
University of Nevada System
405 Marsh Avenue
Reno, Nevada 89502
(702) 784–4901

NEW HAMPSHIRE
New Hampshire Postsecondary
Education Commission
61 South Spring Street
Concord, New Hampshire 03301
(603) 271–2555

NEW JERSEY
Department of Higher
Education
225 West State Street
Trenton, New Jersey 08625
(609) 292–4310

NEW MEXICO
Board of Educational Finance
1068 Cerrillos Road
Santa Fe, New Mexico 87503
(505) 827–2115

NEW YORK
Board of Regents, University
of the State of New York
State Education Department
Albany, New York 12224
(518) 474–5851

NORTH CAROLINA
University of North Carolina
General Administration
Box 2688
Chapel Hill, North
Carolina 27514
(919) 962–6981

NORTH DAKOTA
Board of Higher Education
State Capitol Building
Bismarck, North Dakota 58505
(701) 224–2960

OHIO
Board of Regents
State Office Tower, 36th Floor
30 East Broad Street
Columbus, Ohio 43215
(614) 466–6000

OKLAHOMA
State Regents for Higher
Education
500 Education Building
State Capitol Complex
Oklahoma City, Oklahoma 73105
(405) 521–2444

OREGON
Oregon Educational Coordinating Commission
495 State Street
Salem, Oregon 97310
(503) 378–3921

PENNSYLVANIA
State Department of Education
333 Market Street
Harrisburg, Pennsylvania 17126
(717) 787–5041

PUERTO RICO
Council on Higher Education
Box F-UPR Station
San Juan, Puerto Rico 00931
(809) 765–6590

RHODE ISLAND
Board of Governors for
Higher Education
199 Promenade Street, Suite 208
Providence, Rhode Island 02908
(401) 277–2031

SOUTH CAROLINA
Commission on Higher
Education
1429 Senate Street, Suite 1104
Columbia, South Carolina 29201
(803) 758–2407

SOUTH DAKOTA
The Department of Education
and Cultural Affairs
Richard Kneip Building
Pierre, South Dakota 57501
(605) 773–3455 (Foster)
(605) 773–3134 (Wollman)

TENNESSEE
Tennessee Higher Education
Commission
501 Union Building, #300
Nashville, Tennessee 37219
(615) 741–3605

TEXAS
Coordinating Board, Texas
College and University System
Box 12788, Capitol Station
Austin, Texas 78711
(512) 475–4361

UTAH
State Board of Regents
807 East South Temple, Suite 204
Salt Lake City, Utah 84102
(801) 533–5617

VERMONT
Vermont Higher Education
Planning Commission
Pavilion Office Building
5th Floor
Montepelier, Vermont 05602
(802) 828–2376

VIRGIN ISLANDS
Virgin Islands Commission on
Postsecondary Education
c/o College of the Virgin Islands
St. Thomas, Virgin Islands 00801

VIRGINIA
State Council of Higher
Education
James Monroe Building
101 North Fourteenth Street
Richmond, Virginia 23219
(804) 225-2600

WASHINGTON
Council for Postsecondary
Education
908 East Fifth Street
Olympia, Washington 98504
(206) 753-3241

WEST VIRGINIA
West Virginia Board of Regents
950 Kanawha Boulevard, East
Charleston, West Virginia 25301
(304) 348-2101

WISCONSIN
University of Wisconsin
1700 Van Hise Hall
Madison, Wisconsin 53706
(608) 262-2321

WYOMING
Wyoming Coordinating Council
for Postsecondary Education
c/o Community College
Commission
Boyd Building, 5th Floor
1720 Carey
Cheyenne, Wyoming 82001
(307) 777-7763

BUSINESS/FINANCE MAGAZINES

American Business

Barron's National
Business and Financial
Weekly

Black Enterprise

Changing Times

Consumer Life

Consumer Reports

Consumer's Digest

Fortune Magazine

Inc.

Industry Week

Management Review

Money Magazine

National Business Woman

Parents Magazine

The Secretary

Today's Secretary

Women in Business

Don't let financial aid language put you off. Read through these terms and ask questions to get the information you need.

Key
to
Financial
Aid
Language

This is a glossary of financial aid. If you are like most people, looking into financial aid can seem like learning a whole new language. Many words, phrases, acronyms, titles, and names will probably be unfamiliar. Some of the terms you will need to know are explained below. If you run across one that is not listed, don't give up. Call a financial aid office at a local college or ask a counselor at your public library. The important thing is to ask.

Academic year   A year that is divided into terms or periods of study in several different ways. For example:

1. Semesters are two equal terms, usually from September to June (September to January and February to June).
2. Trimesters are three equal terms, usually from September to June.
3. Quarters are four equal terms, from September to the *next* September. Under this system a student usually completes an academic year by attending three of the four terms.
4. A 4–1–4 calendar has three terms: a four-month term, a one-month term (sometimes called interim or minimester), and another four-month term. The shorter term is often used for a special study project or independent study. *Page 19*

Accelerated program   A college program of study completed in less time than is usually required, most often by attending during summer as well as regular terms or by carrying extra courses. *See page 28 for more information.*

ACT   See *American College Testing Program.*

Adjusted gross income (AGI)   Wages plus other taxable income *minus* exclusions and allowable adjustments to income, following Internal Revenue Service policy. *Page 49*

Admissions tests   See *Scholastic Aptitude Test* (SAT) and *American College Testing* (ACT) *Program Assessment.*

AFDC   See *Aid to Families with Dependent Children.*

Affidavit of Educational Purpose   A document signed by a student who is awarded one or more forms of federal financial aid.

AFSA   See *Application for Federal Student Aid.*

AGI   See *Adjusted gross income.*

Aid index   See *Student Aid Report.*

Aid to Families with Dependent Children (AFDC)   A public assistance program available to families, with children who are minors, who lack adequate means of support because of absence, death, or incapacity of a parent. *Page 67*

ALAS   See *Auxiliary Loans to Assist Services.*

American College Testing (ACT) Program   One of the major national agencies providing admissions and need analysis services to colleges and universities. ACT processes the information on the Family Financial Statement (FFS) to determine student financial need. *Page 16*

American College Testing Program Assessment   The college admissions test battery of the American College Testing Program. *Page 16*

Appeal process   A means by which a student may seek reconsideration of the financial aid award or financial aid application rejection. *Page 42*

Application fee   A nonrefundable fee charged for processing a student's application for admission. Costs vary from college to college, and some will waive the fee at an applicant's request because of financial need. *Page 22*

Application for Federal Student Aid (AFSA)   The form provided by the federal government that may be used to apply for aid. Other forms also available are the FAF, FFS, PHEAA, and SAAC; however, new federal regulations may change forms and procedures. *Page 47*

Assets Savings, checking accounts, home or business value, stocks, bonds, real estate, trust funds. Cars and most personal possessions are not considered assets. *Page 37*

Auxiliary Loans to Assist Students (ALAS) Loans for parents of undergraduate students, independent students, and graduate students (also see *PLUS*). *Page 49*

Award letter A letter from a college's financial aid office explaining the financial aid package that the school is offering a student. It outlines the amount and types of aid that will be awarded. The student must explicitly accept or reject all or part of the award. *Page 38*

Basic Grant Program See *Pell Grant.*

BEOG Program See *Pell Grant.*

Campus-based aid program Federal aid program directly administered by colleges. See *SEOG*; *CW-S*; *NDSL*. *Page 51*

CETA See *Comprehensive Employment and Training Act.*

CLEP See *College-Level Examination Program.*

College-Level Examination Program (CLEP) A credit-by-examination program of the College Board. *Page 26*

College Proficiency Examination Program (CPEP) A credit-by-examination program run by the New York State Education Department and the American College Testing Program. *Page 26*

College Scholarship Service (CSS) of the College Board The major national agency that analyzes financial need. The CSS processes the Financial Aid Form (FAF). *Page 36*

College Work-Study Program (CW-S) One of the three campus-based programs, with 80 percent of the funds provided by the federal government. The remaining 20 percent is provided by the institution, which is responsible for arranging part-time jobs for eligible students, who are paid at least minimum wage. *Page 52*

Commercial loan A loan made through a bank or other lending institution for educational purposes as well as for a house, a car, or other consumer purchases. The interest rate is usually higher than those charged by federal and state student loan programs. *Page 40*

Community college An institution of higher education that usually offers the first two years of college instruction and career education, grants an associate degree, and does not grant a bachelor's degree. Tuition is usually low. *Page 34*

Commuter student One who lives at home and travels to the college. *Page 34*

Comprehensive Employment and Training Act (CETA) A federal program that provides various kinds of job training and opportunities. *Page 64*

Correspondence course A home-study program sent to students and supervised by mail. Limited financial aid is available to cover costs. *Page 32*

CPEP See *College Proficiency Examination Program.*

Credit-by-examination Academic credit granted by a college to a student who has demonstrated proficiency in a subject as measured by an examination. See *College-Level Examination Program* and *College Proficiency Examination Program. Page 26*

Credit for prior learning Award of college credit for completion of formal learning in military service and employment or for previous life and work experience. *Page 27*

CSS See *College Scholarship Service.*

CW-S See *College Work-Study Program.*

Deferred payment An arrangement by which costs can be paid at a later time. Colleges often defer payment of tuition when there is evidence that a student will receive financial aid at a later date. *Page 57*

Dependent A wife, husband, child, parent, or anyone else who receives at least half of his or her support from the student applying for aid. *Page 65*

Dependent student One who lives with and is at least partially supported by parents or a guardian and who is claimed by them as a dependent for income tax purposes or one to whom these conditions applied in the academic year prior to applying for financial aid. *Page 50*

Deposit or advanced preadmission deposit A fee typically charged by colleges and universities to new students. This deposit may range from $100 to $250 and reserves a place at the college for the student. The charge is usually applied to the tuition for the first semester or quarter. Since refund policies vary, check at each college or university you are considering. This deposit is sometimes waived for students who will receive financial aid. Check with the admissions or financial aid office. *See page 33 for more information.*

Educational broker A person who serves as an intermediary, the important go-between for adult learners and the vast array of educational resources. Educational brokers serve adults by providing information, referral, counseling, assessment, and client advocacy. (See page 60 about how to obtain a directory of information.)

Educational costs Expenses related to education, including tuition, fees, books, supplies, room, board, and personal expenses such as laundry, clothing, transportation, meals away from home, and child care. *Page 34*

Emergency loan A small, short-term loan available from many colleges. *Page 57*

External degree A degree earned by taking examinations, transferring credit for courses taken previously, or independent study. *Page 28*

FAF See *Financial Aid Form.*

Family contribution   The amount the family of a dependent student can reasonably be expected to contribute toward educational expenses from income, assets, and student employment. The contribution depends on the family income, the size of the family, the number of family members in postsecondary schools, and unusual expenses. *Page 41*

Family Financial Statement (FFS)   The form used by the American College Testing Program (ACT) to determine a student's need for aid. Students can use the FFS to apply for Pell Grants and other federal, state, and college aid programs at the same time; however, new federal regulations may change procedures for federal programs. *Page 47*

Federally Insured Student Loan (FISL)   See *Guaranteed Student Loan.*

Fees   Expenses in addition to tuition charged by most colleges. Some fees are optional (health insurance fees, for example); others are mandatory. Fees can range from $50 to $200 per term. *Page 33*

FFS   See *Family Financial Statement.*

Financial aid   A general term used to include any money received by a student to help meet college costs. *Page 32*

Financial aid administrator   A college administrator who works in the student financial aid office. *Page 34*

Financial aid application   An institutional form that a student must complete to be considered for financial aid. This form is in addition to applications for admission. *Page 36*

Financial Aid Form (FAF)   The form used by the College Scholarship Service of the College Board to determine a student's need for financial aid. Students can use the FAF to apply for Pell Grants and other federal, state, and college aid programs at the same time; however, new federal regulations may change the procedure for federal programs. *Page 36*

Financial aid package   The total amount of financial aid a student receives. Federal and nonfederal aid such as loans, grants, or work study are combined to help meet the student's need. *See the chart on page 96.*

Financial need   The difference between what it costs to study and what you are determined to be able to pay. Various aid programs determine financial need in different ways. *Page 38*

FISL   Federally Insured Student Loan. See *Guaranteed Student Loan.*

Full-time student   One who takes at least 12 credit hours each semester or the equivalent. *Page 40*

Grant   A type of financial aid that does not have to be repaid. It is awarded according to financial need. *Page 32*

Gross income   The total income of a family, including salaries, wages, interest, social security benefits, and any other taxable and nontaxable income. *Page 66*

GSL   See *Guaranteed Student Loan.*

Guaranteed Student Loan (GSL)   Federally Insured Student Loan. The federal government will pay the interest on a GSL that you obtain through a bank or other lending institution. To qualify you must be enrolled in a degree program at least half-time. *Page 49*

Half-time student   Usually a student who takes at least six credit hours each semester or the equivalent. Students must be enrolled at least half time to receive most student aid. Institutional definitions of half-time students vary. *Page 40*

Independent or private college   A postsecondary institution that is under one of a variety of forms of private control, is governed by an independent board of trustees, and whose major source of funds is other than public funds. *Page 29*

Independent student   One who is not financially dependent on any other person, except a spouse, for support. *Page 50*

Installment payment plan Plan that enables students to pay tuition and fee payments over a period of time. *Page 57*

Junior college A postsecondary institution that offers the first two years of college instruction, frequently confers an associate degree and does not confer a bachelor's degree. The term "junior college" is often used interchangeably with the term "community college." *Page 51*

Matriculation Formal enrollment of a student in a degree or certificate program. *Page 15*

National Direct Student Loan (NDSL) Program One of three federal campus-based programs through which funds can be borrowed. *Page 52*

NDSL See *National Direct Student Loan Program.*

Need See *Financial need.*

Need analysis A system or formula that estimates a student's ability to pay the costs of education. See *Family Financial Statement (FFS)* and *Financial Aid Form (FAF). Page 37*

Nontaxable income Income not included on tax return forms, such as social security, welfare, unemployment benefits, and any other social service help. *Page 69*

Part-time student Takes less than the full-time course load per semester as defined by the institution. *Page 40*

Pell Grant A federal student aid program for undergraduates. Formerly called a Basic Educational Opportunity Grant or BEOG. *Page 46*

Pennsylvania Higher Education Assistance Application (PHEAA) One of five forms that may be used to apply for a Pell Grant, state grant assistance, and, in some situations, campus-based aid; however, new federal regulations may change the procedure for federal programs. It can be used by residents of Pennsylvania applying for state grants, and for additional aid at some Pennsylvania institutions. *Page 47*

PHEAA   See *Pennsylvania Higher Education Assistance Application.*

PLUS   An auxiliary loan program for parents of undergraduate students, independent undergraduate students, and graduate students. (See also *ALAS*). *Page 49*

Postsecondary institution   Any proprietary or vocational school, college, or university that offers education and training to students beyond the high school level. *Page 34*

Proprietary school   A postsecondary institution operated for profit. *Page 32*

Public institution   Any college, university, or vocational school that is supported primarily by public funds and is operated by publicly appointed or elected officials who control its programs and activities. *Page 29*

SAAC   See *Student Aid Application for California.*

Sallie Mae   A government-chartered, stockholder-owned corporation that provides a national secondary market for student loans under the Guaranteed Student Loan Program made by financial and educational institutions, state agencies, and other organizations. *Page 110*

SAI   See *Student Aid Index.*

SAR   See *Student Aid Report.*

SAT   See *Scholastic Aptitude Test.*

Satisfactory academic progress   An eligibility requirement for most aid programs. To continue to receive financial aid, students must successfully complete courses according to the standards of the institution. *Page 39*

Scholarship   An outright award that does not have to be repaid. *Page 32*

Scholastic Aptitude Test (SAT)   The College Board's college admission test of verbal and mathematical reasoning abilities. *Page 16*

Self-help The amount of money that a student and spouse are expected to pay for college costs. For most adults, this is similar to the family contribution. Self-help expectations vary with each institution. *See the chart on page 96.*

Self-supporting student See *Independent student.*

SEOG See *Supplemental Educational Opportunity Grant Program.*

Short-term loan A loan from a college that must be repaid by the end of the semester or quarter. Usually it is interest free. *Page 57*

Student Aid Application for California (SAAC) One of five forms that may be used to apply for a Pell Grant and campus-based aid; however, new federal regulations may change the procedure for federal programs. *Page 47*

Student Aid Index (SAI) A number on an individual's student aid report (SAR) used by an educational institution to determine the size of the Pell Grant awarded. *Page 48*

Student Aid Report (SAR) The notification received after an application for a Pell Grant has been processed. This report includes an eligibility index that indicates whether or not the applicant can receive a grant. *Page 48*

Student expense budget The annual cost of attending college, which usually includes tuition, fees, books and supplies, personal expenses, and the expenses of living at home or for room and board at college. Additional expenses for dependent children or a spouse may be included, as well as the educational costs related to assisting a disabled student attending a postsecondary institution. *Page 35*

Supplemental Educational Opportunity Grant (SEOG) **Program** One of three federal campus-based programs. *Page 52*

Taxable income Income included on tax returns: salaries, wages, tips, interest, and dividends minus deductions and exemptions. *Page 69*

Tuition   The cost charged by colleges or institutions for courses in which the student enrolls. *Page 33*

Undergraduate   A student enrolled in a postsecondary institution who has not yet received a bachelor's degree. *Page 33*

Uniform methodology   The federal need analysis system generally used by the American College Testing Program, the College Scholarship Service, the Pennsylvania Higher Education Assistance Application, the Student Aid Application for California, and the United States Department of Education to determine eligibility for campus-based funds. *See page 37 for more information.*

United States Department of Education, Bureau of Student Financial Assistance   The federal department that administers the five major federal student aid programs. *Page 41*

Unmet need   The difference between your educational costs and your total financial aid package. See *Financial aid. Page 97*

WIN   See *Work Incentive Program.*

Work Incentive Program (WIN)   A public assistance program administered through state agencies. *Page 64*

Work-Study Program   See *College Work-Study Program.*

Familiarize yourself with these forms.
You will have to use similar forms
when you apply for financial aid.

12

1982–83
Financial
Aid
Form
and
CSS
Worksheet

financial Aid form
School Year 1982-83

COLLEGE SCHOLARSHIP SERVICE OF THE COLLEGE BOARD

What is the Financial Aid Form?

The Financial Aid Form (FAF) is a form that you fill out if you want to apply for financial aid for the school year 1982-83 from:

- financial aid programs at colleges where you are thinking of going after high school or where you now go
- state scholarship and grant programs
- federal student financial aid programs, including the Pell (Basic) Grant Program

The information you give on the FAF is confidential.

After you complete the FAF, send it to the College Scholarship Service (CSS). The CSS will analyze it and send the information to the colleges and programs that you list on your FAF. Each college or program then decides whether you will get financial aid and how much aid you will get.

How do I apply for financial aid from colleges and from state scholarship and grant programs?

Check with the colleges you want to attend and your state scholarship or grant program to see if they need a copy of the FAF. If so, list them in question 41. It costs $6.50 for the first college or program and $4.50 for each other college or program you list in question 41. Don't send cash. Make your check or money order out to the College Scholarship Service. Some colleges and programs may ask you to fill out other forms as well.

How do I apply for federal student financial aid programs?

You apply for federal student financial aid programs by checking "Yes" in question 43. You'll find more information about federal student financial aid programs in this booklet.

When should I fill out the FAF?

Fill out and mail the FAF after January 1, 1982, but at least one month before the earliest deadline of the colleges and programs that you list in question 41. Don't file this FAF after March 15, 1983.

What is my CSS "Estimated Contribution"?

The CSS estimates what you and your family can pay toward your costs for college. Remember that each college or program makes the final decision about how much you and your family can pay. Because of this, the amount that the college or program figures can be higher or lower than the CSS Estimated Contribution.

The CSS will send you a report showing the information that was used to calculate your estimated contribution.

Where do I send the FAF?

After you fill out the FAF, put it in the envelope that you'll find inside this booklet and mail it to the correct address given below.

If you live in:

Alabama	AL	New Hampshire	NH
Connecticut	CT	New Jersey	NJ
Delaware	DE	New York	NY
District of		North Carolina	NC
Columbia	DC	Ohio	OH
Florida	FL	Pennsylvania	PA
Georgia	GA	Puerto Rico	PR
Indiana	IN	Rhode Island	RI
Kentucky	KY	South Carolina	SC
Louisiana	LA	Tennessee	TN
Maine	ME	Vermont	VT
Maryland	MD	Virgin Is	VI
Massachusetts	MA	Virginia	VA
Michigan	MI	West Virginia	WV
Mississippi	MS	Wisconsin	WI

send your filled-out FAF to:

College Scholarship Service
Box 2700
Princeton, NJ 08541

If you live in:

Alaska	AK	Nevada	NV
Amer. Samoa	AS	New Mexico	NM
Arizona	AZ	North Dakota	ND
Arkansas	AR	Northern	
California	CA	Mariana Is.	CM
Colorado	CO	Oklahoma	OK
Guam	GU	Oregon	OR
Hawaii	HI	South Dakota	SD
Idaho	ID	Texas	TX
Illinois	IL	Trust Territory of	
Iowa	IA	the Pacific Is.	
Kansas	KS	(Marshall and	
Minnesota	MN	Caroline Is.)	TT
Missouri	MO	Utah	UT
Montana	MT	Washington	WA
Nebraska	NE	Wyoming	WY

send your filled-out FAF to:

College Scholarship Service
Box 380
Berkeley, CA 94701

If you live somewhere other than the places listed above, send your filled-out FAF to the CSS office in Princeton, NJ.

Will the CSS tell me when it has finished analyzing my FAF?

Yes. The CSS will send you an Acknowledgment after it has analyzed your FAF. The Acknowledgment (including your "Estimated Contribution") will be sent to the student's mailing address given in question 2 of the FAF.

The Acknowledgment will list the colleges and programs to which your FAF was sent. If you list more than six colleges to get your FAF, the Acknowledgment will list only the first six. A second Acknowledgment will be sent to you separately which will list the additional colleges.

What if I later want to send my FAF to another college or program?

The Acknowledgment form has a section which you can tear off and send to CSS if you later want to send your FAF to another college or program. The section is called the Additional College Request Form (ACR). The fee for the ACR is $6.50 for the first college or program you list and $4.50 for each other one.

Note: Some colleges and programs may ask you to send a copy of your income tax return to them. If so, send it directly to the college or program. If you don't give the income tax information that is asked for, you may not receive aid. **Don't send any income tax forms with your FAF to the CSS.**

Financial aid for your college education can come from the federal government, your state government, your college, and privately sponsored programs. Financial aid can include grants (money you don't have to pay back), loans, and jobs. This information should help you understand more about the federal student financial aid programs.

FEDERAL STUDENT FINANCIAL AID PROGRAMS

You can use this form as the first step in applying for financial aid from five student assistance programs offered by the U.S. Department of Education (ED). More than 6,500 colleges and other institutions take part in one or more of the federal programs. Some colleges, however, do not take part in all of the programs. Contact the college financial aid administrator to find out which federal programs the college participates in.

What are the five federal student aid programs?

Pell Grants (formerly called Basic Grants) Pell Grants are awarded to students who need money to pay for college. A Pell Grant is not a loan, so you don't have to pay it back. To get a Pell Grant, you must go to college at least half-time and be an undergraduate who doesn't already have a bachelor's degree.

Supplemental Educational Opportunity Grants (SEOG) An SEOG is also a grant. To get an SEOG, you must be an undergraduate who doesn't already have a bachelor's degree. Usually, you must be going to college at least half-time. However, a college can award SEOGs to a limited number of students who are enrolled for less than half-time.

College Work-Study (CWS) A CWS job lets you earn part of your college expenses for either undergraduate or graduate study. Usually, you must be going to college at least half-time. However, a college can award CWS jobs to a limited number of students who are enrolled for less than half-time.

National Direct Student Loans (NDSL) NDSLs are low-interest loans made by a college to both undergraduate and graduate students who are going to college at least half-time. After you leave college, you must repay this money.

Guaranteed Student Loans (GSL) A GSL is a low-interest loan made to you by a lender such as a bank, credit union, or savings and loan association. These loans are for both undergraduate and graduate students who are going to college at least half-time. After you leave college, you must repay this money.

Who can get aid from these programs?

To receive financial aid from these federal programs, you must:
* Be a U.S. citizen or an eligible noncitizen.
* Have financial need. The ED and your college will use the information you put on this form to determine your need.
* Attend a college that takes part in one or more of the programs.
* Be enrolled and working toward a degree, diploma, or certificate.

How do I get aid from these programs?

Fill out the FAF, check "Yes" to question 43, and send it to the CSS with the correct fee. **Your form must be received by March 15, 1983 but not before January 1, 1982. The sooner you send it in, the better.** The CSS will send your information to the ED.

Within six weeks after you mail in this form, the ED will send you a *Student Aid Report* (SAR). On the SAR will be a number called a *Student Aid Index* (SAI). A formula established by law is used to figure this number. The SAI helps decide whether you can get a Pell Grant and, if so, how much. The lower the SAI, the higher the Pell Grant will be. This SAI will also help the college decide whether you are eligible for aid from the SEOG, NDSL, and CWS programs.

If you don't get a SAR within six weeks, write to: Federal Student Aid Programs, Box 92505, Los Angeles, CA 90000. Give your name, address, social security number, and date of birth, and ask for a copy of your SAR. If your address has changed since you sent in your FAF, be sure to give your old and new addresses.

What if my financial situation changes?

This form asks mostly about income and expenses for 1981. If your financial situation has recently changed for the worse, you may be able to fill out a Special Condition Application for Federal Student Aid. That application asks mostly about the income and expenses that you expect to have in 1982. Contact your financial aid administrator to find out more about the Special Condition Application for Federal Student Aid.

Where can I get additional information?

Write to Federal Student Aid Programs, Box 84, Washington, DC 20044, and ask for a copy of *The Student Guide: Five Federal Financial Aid Programs, 1982-83.*

Information on the Privacy Act and Use of Your Social Security Number

The Privacy Act of 1974 says that each federal agency that asks for your social security number or other information must tell you:
* its legal right to ask for the information and whether the law says you must give it
* what purpose the agency has in asking for it and how it will be used
* what could happen if you do not give it

You must give your social security number in order to apply for a Pell Grant and a Guaranteed Student Loan. The social security number is needed to know who you are, to process your form, and to keep track of your record. In addition, your social security number is used in the Pell Grant Program in recording information about your college attendance and progress; in making payments to you directly in case your college doesn't handle this, and in making sure that you have received your money. If you don't give your social security number, you will not get a Pell Grant or a Guaranteed Student Loan.

The legal right to require that you provide your social security number for the Pell Grant and Guaranteed Student Loan programs is based on Section 7(a) (2) of the Privacy Act of 1974.

It is requested that you voluntarily give your social security number if you are using this form only to apply for financial aid from the College Work-Study, National Direct Student Loan, and Supplemental Educational Opportunity Grant programs. Your social security number is used in processing your form. If you don't give your social security number, you are not disqualified from receiving aid under these programs.

The legal right to ask for all information except your social security number is based on sections of the law that authorizes the Pell Grant, Supplemental Educational Opportunity Grant, College Work-Study, National Direct Student Loan, and Guaranteed Student Loan programs. These include sections 411, 413B, 443, 464, 425, 428, and 482 of the Higher Education Act of 1965, as amended.

If you apply or intend to apply for student aid under all five programs, you must fill in all parts of the application except questions 30, 41, 42, 44, and all of Side II. However, if you are not applying or intending to apply for a Guaranteed Student Loan, you need not answer questions 7 and 16 as well as questions 30, 41, 42, 44, and all of Side II. Finally, if you are not applying for a Pell Grant or a Supplemental Educational Opportunity Grant, you need not answer question 8 as well as questions 30, 41, 42, 44, and all of Side II. If you don't answer question 44, it will be counted as "No."

The information on the form is asked for so that your Student Aid Index can be figured. The Student Aid Index is used to help decide how much federal financial aid you will get, if any. If you don't give the required information, you will not get federal student financial aid.

Your name, address, social security number, date of birth, Student Aid Indexes, student status, year in college, and state of legal residence will be sent to the first two colleges you list in question 41 even if you check "No" in question 44. This information will also go to the state scholarship agency in your state of legal residence to help it coordinate state financial aid programs with federal student aid programs. Also, information may be sent to members of Congress if you or your parents ask them to help with federal student aid questions. The information also may be used for any purpose which is a "routine use" listed in Appendix B of 34 CFR 5b.

Financial Aid Form—Side I

School Year 1982-83

Read the instructions carefully as you fill in this form.

Section A—Student's Information

Warning

If you use this form to establish eligibility for federal student aid funds, you should know that any person who makes false statements or misrepresentations on this form is subject to a fine or to imprisonment or both, under provisions of the United States Criminal Code.

1. Student's name
   Last | First | M.I.

2. Student's permanent mailing address (See front cover for state abbreviation.)
   Number, street, and apartment number
   City | State | Zip code

3. Student's social security number

4. Student's date of birth
   Month | Day | Year

5. Student's state of legal residence
   State

6. The student is
   1 ☐ a U.S. citizen
   2 ☐ an eligible noncitizen (See instructions.)
   3 ☐ neither of the above (See instructions.)

7. Student's year in **college** during 1982-83. (Check only one box.)
   1 ☐ 1st (freshman)   5 ☐ 5th (undergraduate)
   2 ☐ 2nd (sophomore)   6 ☐ beginning graduate or professional (beyond a bachelor's degree)
   3 ☐ 3rd (junior)   7 ☐ continuing graduate or professional
   4 ☐ 4th (senior)

8. Will the student have a bachelor's degree by July 1, 1982?   Yes ☐ 1   No ☐ 2

9. The student is   1 ☐ unmarried (single, divorced, or widowed)
                    2 ☐ married
                    3 ☐ separated

10. How many dependent children does the student have? (If none, write in "0".)

Section B—Student's Status
Read the instructions to find out who counts as the student's parent before you answer 11, 12, and 13.

		Yes	No		Yes	No
11.	Did or will the student live with the parents for more than six weeks (42 days)	..in 1981? 1 ☐ 2 ☐		..in 1982?	1 ☐ 2 ☐	
12.	Did or will the parents claim the student as an income tax exemption	..in 1981? 1 ☐ 2 ☐		..in 1982?	1 ☐ 2 ☐	
13.	Did or will the student get more than $750 worth of support from the parents	..in 1981? 1 ☐ 2 ☐		..in 1982?	1 ☐ 2 ☐	

If you answered "Yes" to any of the questions in Section B, you must fill in the blue shaded areas.
- Exception: If you are married, fill in both the blue and the gray shaded areas.
- If your parents are separated or divorced, if your parent is widowed or single, or if you have a stepparent, you must read the instructions before going on.

If you answered "No" to all 6 questions in Section B, you must fill in the gray shaded areas. Some colleges or programs may also ask you to fill in the blue shaded areas.

Section C—Household Information

Parents

14. The parents' current marital status is:
    1 ☐ single   3 ☐ separated   5 ☐ widowed
    2 ☐ married   4 ☐ divorced

15. The parents' state of legal residence is

16. The age of the older parent is

17. The total size of the parents' household during 1982-83 will be (Include the student even if he/she does not live at home. Also include parents and parents' other dependent children. Include other people only if they meet the definition in the instructions.)

18. Of the number in 17, how many will be in college during 1982-83? (Include the student who is applying for aid and others who will be in college at least half-time.)

Student (and spouse)

19. The total size of the student's household during 1982-83 will be (Include the student, spouse, and student's dependent children. Include other people only if they meet the definition in the instructions.)

20. Of the number in 19, how many will be in college during 1982-83? (Include the student who is applying for aid and others who will be in college at least half-time.)

Section D—Income and Expense Information

- If you will file or have filed a 1981 U.S. income tax return, go to 21.
- If you will not file a 1981 U.S. income tax return, skip to 26.

		Parents	Student (and spouse)
21.	The following 1981 U.S. income tax return figures are (See instructions.)	1 ☐ from a completed return 2 ☐ estimated	21. 1 ☐ from a completed return 2 ☐ estimated
22.	1981 total number of exemptions (IRS Form 1040, line 6e or 1040A, line 6)		22.
23.	1981 income from IRS Form 1040, line 31 or 1040A, line 10 (Use the worksheet in the instructions.)	$ .00	23. $ .00
24. a.	1981 U.S. income tax paid (IRS Form 1040, line 47 or 1040A, line 15a)	$ .00	24a. $ .00
b.	1981 state and local income taxes paid	$ .00	24b. $ .00
25.	1981 itemized deductions (IRS Form 1040, Schedule A, line 39. Write in "0" if deductions were not itemized.)	$ .00	25. $ .00
26.	1981 income earned from work by	a. Father $ .00 b. Mother $ .00	26a. Student $ .00 26b. Spouse $ .00
27.	1981 other income and benefits a. Social security benefits (Don't include the student's benefits.)	$ .00	27a. XXXXXXXXXXXX
	b. Aid to Families with Dependent Children (AFDC or ADC)	$ .00	27b. $ .00
	c. All other 1981 income and benefits (child support, disability income, etc.) (Use the worksheet in the instructions.)	$ .00	27c. $ .00

Tax Filers Only

Section D—Income and Expense Information (continued)

		Parents	Student (and spouse)
28.	1981 medical and dental expenses not paid by insurance	$ .00	28. $ .00
29.	1981 elementary, junior high, and high school tuition paid (Don't include tuition paid for the student.)	$ .00	29. $ .00
30.	Expected 1982 taxable and nontaxable income and benefits (See instructions.)	$ .00	If you are filling in only the gray shaded areas, skip to Section E. Don't answer 30, 31, and 32.

If you are filling in the blue shaded areas, answer 31 and 32 about the student. Use the worksheets in the instructions to figure out the answers.

31.	Student's (and spouse's) total 1981 income minus U.S., state, and local income taxes paid	$ .00	
32.	Student's (and spouse's) savings and net assets	$ .00	

Section E—Asset Information

		Parents		Student (and spouse)	
		What is it worth now?	What is owed on it?	What is it worth now?	What is owed on it?
33.	Cash, savings, and checking accounts	$ .00		$ .00	
34.	Home (Renters write in "0".)	$ .00	$ .00	$ .00	$ .00
35.	Other real estate and investments	$ .00	$ .00	$ .00	$ .00
36.	Business and farm	$ .00	$ .00	$ .00	$ .00

ALL STUDENTS MUST FILL IN SECTIONS F AND G.

Section F—Student's (and Spouse's) Expected Income and Benefits

		Summer 1982	School Year 1982-83
37.	a. Student's taxable income (Don't include student financial aid.)	3 months $ .00	9 months $ .00
	b. Spouse's taxable income (Don't include student financial aid.)	3 months $ .00	9 months $ .00

July 1, 1982–June 30, 1983

38.	Social security benefits (for student, spouse, and dependent children)	Amount per month $ .00	Number of months
39.	Veterans educational benefits (Include only the student's benefits from the GI Bill and Dependents Educational Assistance Program. Don't include VA Contributory Benefits.)	Amount per month $ .00	Number of months
40.	Other income and benefits of student (and spouse) (Don't include student financial aid or any of the income or benefits given in 37, 38, and 39.)	Amount for July 1, 1982–June 30, 1983 $ .00	

Section G—Other Information and Signatures

41. List the names and code numbers of the colleges and programs that are to get information from this FAF. **Don't list** federal student aid programs. Be sure you enclose the right fee.

Name	City and state	CSS Code No.	★

★ Housing Codes:
1 = Campus residence hall
2 = Campus married student housing
3 = Parents' home
4 = Relatives' home
5 = Off-campus residence hall
6 = Off-campus apartment/house
7 = Other type of housing

42. Fee: Check the box next to the number of colleges and programs listed in 41.

1 ☐ $6.50   3 ☐ $15.50   5 ☐ $24.50
2 ☐ $11.00   4 ☐ $20.00   6 ☐ $29.00

Mail this FAF with a check or money order for the right amount made out to the College Scholarship Service.

43. Do you give CSS permission to send information from this FAF to the U.S. Department of Education? (Answer "Yes" if you want to be considered for the Pell (Basic) Grant, Supplemental Educational Opportunity Grant, College Work-Study, National Direct Student Loan, or Guaranteed Student Loan programs.)

Yes ☐ 1   No ☐ 2

44. Do you give the U.S. Department of Education permission to send information from this FAF to:

a. the financial aid agency in your state?   Yes ☐ 1   No ☐ 2
b. the first two colleges in 41?   Yes ☐ 1   No ☐ 2

Note: Answering "Yes" to **44a** and **44b** will not meet the requirements of most states and colleges for applying for financial aid. See instructions.

Certification: All of the information on this form is true and complete to the best of my knowledge. If asked by an authorized official, I agree to give proof of the information that I have given on this form. I realize that this proof may include a copy of my 1981 U.S., state, or local income tax return. I also realize that if I don't give proof when asked, the student may not get aid.

1 _____   2 _____
Student's signature   Spouse's signature

3 _____   4 _____
Father's signature   Mother's signature

Date completed:
Month Day Year

CONTINUE WITH QUESTION 46 ON THE NEXT PAGE. ➡

Financial Aid Form—Side II
School Year 1982-83

Section H—Student's Information (continued)

46. Student's name
Last — First — M.I.

47. Student's home telephone number
Area Code — Number

48. Student's sex (optional)   1 ☐ Male   2 ☐ Female

49. If an entering first-time student during 1982-83, enter your high school 6-digit code number. Otherwise, leave blank.
Code Number

Name of high school _____

50. Expected college degree or certificate
_____

Student's expected date of completion of college degree or certificate
Month — Year

51. For what academic period(s) in 1982-83 does the student want financial assistance? (Check all boxes that apply.)
1 ☐ Academic year, 1982-83   4 ☐ Winter term, 1982-83
2 ☐ Summer term, 1982   5 ☐ Spring term, 1983
3 ☐ Fall term, 1982   6 ☐ Summer term, 1983

Section I—Parents' Information

52. Breakdown of income in 23.

	1981	Estimated 1982
a. Wages, salaries, tips—father or stepfather	$ .00	$ .00
b. Wages, salaries, tips—mother or stepmother	$ .00	$ .00
c.-d. Interest and dividend income after IRS exclusion	$ .00	$ .00
e. Net income (or loss) from business or farm. If a loss, enter the amount in (parentheses).	$ .00	$ .00
f. Other taxable income, such as capital gains (or losses), pensions, annuities, rents, royalties, partnerships, estates, trusts, etc. (List in 69.)	$ .00	$ .00
g. Adjustments to income (Give only IRS allowable amounts. See the worksheet in the instructions for 23. List in 69.)	$ .00	$ .00

53. Other income and benefits

	1981	Estimated 1982
a. Social security benefits	$ .00	$ .00
b. Aid to Families with Dependent Children (AFDC or ADC)	$ .00	$ .00
c. All other income and benefits (List in 69.)	$ .00	$ .00

54. Check one box: ☐ father   ☐ stepfather   ☐ guardian
a. Name _____
b. Street address _____
c. City/State/Zip _____
d. Occupation/Title _____
e. Employer _____   f. Number of years _____
g. Social security number ___ — __ — ____

55. Check one box: ☐ mother   ☐ stepmother   ☐ guardian
a. Name _____
b. Street address _____
c. City/State/Zip _____
d. Occupation/Title _____
e. Employer _____   f. Number of years _____
g. Social security number ___ — __ — ____

56. Monthly home mortgage or rental payment (If none, explain in 69.) $ .00

57. If you own a home, give
a. year purchased _____   b. purchase price $ .00

58. If you included investments or other real estate in 35, list

	What is it worth now?	What is owed on it?
a. investments	$ .00	$ .00
b. other real estate	$ .00	$ .00

59. Give information for all children and other dependents who are included in parents' household in 17. Include parent if he or she will attend college in 1982-83. For persons not in school, give name and age only. If you need extra space, continue in 69.

		Educational information 1981-82						Educational information 1982-83			
Name	Age	Name of school or college	Year in school or college	Tuition and fees	Room and board	Scholarships and gift aid	Parents' contribution	Name of school or college	full-time	half-time or more	less than half-time
Student applicant											

(Check appropriate box if attending college)

60. Divorced or separated parents
(To be completed by the parent who has filed this form)

a. Student's natural or adoptive parents are:
☐ Divorced
☐ Legally separated
☐ Separated—no court action
Date of divorce or separation — Month — Year

b. Other parent's name _____
Home address _____
Occupation/Title _____
Employer _____

c. According to court order, when will support for student end? — Month — Year

	1981	Estimated 1982
d. Amount of child support received for the student	$ .00	$ .00
e. Total amount of child support received for all children	$ .00	$ .00
f. Amount of alimony received by parent who filed this form	$ .00	$ .00
g. Is there any agreement specifying a contribution for student's education? Yes ☐ No ☐ If yes, how much per year?	$ .00	$ .00

h. Who claimed student as a tax dependent for 1981? _____

i. If there are special circumstances, check here ☐ and explain in 69.

Section J—Student's Additional Information

61. Student's (and spouse's) resources
(Don't enter monthly amounts.)

	Summer 1982 (3 months)	Academic Year 1982-83 (9 months)
a. Student's wages, salaries, tips, etc. (before taxes and deductions. Don't include work-study earnings.)	$ .00	$ .00
b. Spouse's wages, salaries, tips, etc. (before taxes and deductions. Don't include work-study earnings.)	$ .00	$ .00
c. Other taxable income (interest, dividends, etc.)	$ .00	$ .00
d. Social security benefits	$ .00	$ .00
e. Veterans benefits	$ .00	$ .00
f. Aid to Families with Dependent Children (AFDC or ADC)	$ .00	$ .00
g. Support from student's parents ▶	$ .00	$ .00
h. Support from spouse's parents	$ .00	$ .00
i. Grants, scholarships, fellowships, loans, and other aid already awarded (**List in 69.**)	$ .00	$ .00
j. Other nontaxable income	$ .00	$ .00
k. Total resources	$ .00	$ .00

62. Student's

a. Occupation _____

b. Employer _____

63. Spouse's

a. Name _____ b. Age _____

c. Occupation _____

d. Employer _____

e. College in 1982-83 _____

64. Give information for all children and other dependents.

Name	Age

65. Monthly home mortgage or rental payment (If none, explain in **69.**) $ .00

66. If you own a home, give

a. year purchased _____ b. purchase price $ .00

67. If you included investments or other real estate in 35, list

	What is it worth now?	What is owed on it?
a. investments	$ .00	$ .00
b. other real estate	$ .00	$ .00

68. List all colleges attended since high school up to and including the present. If you need more space, continue in **69.**

Name of college	City and state	Period of attendance (mo./yr. to mo./yr.)	Check if you received financial aid.	CSS Code Number

Section K—Explanations and Special Circumstances

69. Use this space to list types and amounts of income or expense for questions **52f, 52g, 53c,** and **61i.** Also explain any unusual expenses, educational and other debts, or special circumstances. **If you give an explanation below or on additional sheets of paper, check here.** ⟶ ☐

Meeting College Costs Worksheet for Self-Supporting Students

The purpose of this sheet is to help you determine whether you might be eligible for financial aid—grants, loans, and student employment.

Most colleges and other organizations that award financial aid believe parents and students have a responsibility to pay as much as they can toward education costs. The back of this sheet shows the CSS method used in estimating the financial need of students who are considered to be self-supporting.

Specific criteria have been developed for the purpose of determining who should be classified as dependent on their parents and who can be considered independent or self-supporting. If a student satisfies these criteria, he or she might not be required to supply parents' financial data when applying for financial aid. Some institutions, however, require that parental information be supplied by all applicants seeking aid regardless of the student's dependency status.

Most institutions consider the following factors in defining an independent student: the student's age, length of time away from the parents' home, whether the student has been claimed as a dependent for tax purposes, and the amount of support the student receives from parents. The definition set forth by the CSS for students applying for aid in 1983-84 is that for the years 1982 and 1983, the applicant (1) must not live with parents more than six weeks a year; (2) must not be listed by parents as a federal income tax exemption; (3) must not receive more than $750 in parental support.

If a student completing a Financial Aid Form meets these criteria, the CSS uses the procedure on the reverse side to analyze the student's ability to pay for education costs. A simple outline such as this cannot provide the exact determination of financial need that a college or aid program will make, but it does give a rough estimate of what contribution may be expected from a student's resources. Aid decisions are made by individual institutions and scholarship programs—not by the CSS.

If you find that you cannot meet the total education costs with your available resources, you should apply for financial aid. Ask each institution that you are considering about its application procedures.

Estimating What Self-Supporting Students May be Asked to Pay

	Student	Denise Single student, age 21, who works part time	Edward Married graduate student, age 30, with two children
A. Total student expenses		$ 4,990	$ 7,750
Income (for 12-month period including enrollment)			
1. Your wages, salaries, tips, and other compensation		1,845	1,200
2. Spouse's wages, salaries, tips, and other compensation		0	3,800
3. All other taxable income (dividends, interest, etc.)		0	0
4. Financial assistance from parents		150	0
5. Social security benefits, veterans' benefits, and other non-taxable income		0	0
B. Total income (Add 1, 2, 3, 4, and 5)		1,995	5,000
Expenses			
6. U.S. income tax you expect to pay on the above income (not the amount withheld from paycheck)		0	0
7. Social security (FICA) tax (6.7 percent times each salary to a maximum of $2,170 each)		123	334
8. State and local taxes (Enter 4 percent of B)		79	200
C. Total expenses (Add 6, 7, and 8)		202	534
D. Available income (Subtract C from B)		1,793	4,466
Assets			
9. Home equity (total estimated value of your home on the current market less any unpaid balance on your mortgage)		0	9,500
10. Cash, savings, and checking accounts		300	500
11. Other investments and real estate equity (current value)		0	0

E. Total assets (Add 9, 10, and 11)	300	10,000
Deductions		
F. Asset protection allowance (See Table for F)	0	8,200
G. Remaining assets (Subtract F from E)	300	1,800
H. Contribution from assets (Multiply G by 35 percent)	105	630
I. Student's resources (Add D and H)	1,898	5,096
J. Student's need (Subtract I from A)	$ 3,092	$ 2,654

Table for F. Asset protection allowance

Student's age	Student's family size	
	Two or more	One
25 or less	$ 0	$ 0
26	1,600	1,300
27	3,300	2,600
28	4,900	4,000
29	6,600	5,300
30	8,200	6,600
31	9,800	7,900
32	11,500	9,200
33	13,100	10,600
34	14,800	11,900
35	16,400	13,200
36	18,000	14,500
37	19,700	15,800
38	21,300	17,200
39	23,000	18,500
40 or more	24,600	19,800

Copyright © 1983 by College Entrance Examination Board. All rights reserved.
Printed in the United States of America.

2191940 • Y102P2 • Printed in U.S.A.

CARL CAMPBELL BRIGHAM LIBRARY
EDUCATIONAL TESTING SERVICE
PRINCETON, NEW JERSEY 08540